VERGE 2011

THE UNKNOWABLE

A COLLABORATION BETWEEN

 MONASH University

AND

THE UNIVERSITY OF
WARWICK

VERGE 2011

THE UNKNOWABLE

EDITED BY
Anna MacDonald
Bethany Norris
Catherine Noske
Nicholas Tipple

MONASH University
Publishing

Monash University Publishing
Building 4, Monash University
Clayton, Victoria 3800, Australia
www.publishing.monash.edu

This book is available online at
www.publishing.monash.edu/verge

ISBN: 978-1-921867-20-0 (pb)
ISBN: 978-1-921867-21-7 (web)

Monash University Publishing brings to the world publications which advance the best traditions of humane and enlightened thought.

Monash University Publishing titles pass through a rigorous process of independent peer review.

Referees: Associate Professor Anne Brewster (University of New South Wales), Dr Elin-Maria Evangelista (Monash University), Dr Melinda Harper (Monash University), Professor Trevor Harris (Université François-Rabelais), Dr John Hawke (Monash University), Professor Sue Kossew (Monash University), Professor Lyn Mccredden (Deakin University), Dr Helen MacDonald (University of Melbourne), Professor Stephen Muecke (University of New South Wales), Dr Simone Murray (Monash University), Dr Tom Petsinis (Victoria University), and Associate Professor Kate Rigby (Monash University).

Cover design: Les Thomas
Cover artwork © 2011 Peter Blegvad

Printed in Australia by Griffin Press an Accredited ISO AS/NZS 14001:2004 Environmental Management System printer.

CONTENTS

Foreword

Dr Michael Hulse

EZRA POUND RE-TELLS in the *ABC of Reading* the story of Flaubert teaching Maupassant to write by requiring him to describe a concierge they would meet on their next walk in such a way that Flaubert could not mistake her for some other concierge. In the glory days of realism, it appears, writers did things differently. Not just that they must have talked to a lot of concierges, for fear that their learning exercises prove pointless. They must also have valued empirical precision above all other writerly qualities.

Yes – getting it right, caring about seeing and knowing and recording things as they are, is a crux. If a writer can't care about this, what on earth can she/he care about? 'You should not be able to lose a thirty-acre field in such a well-spaced city,' says a tourist, searching. What she finds is 'a stretch of blank concrete space, the kind my eyes are used to editing out. But I can see it now: long, empty, paved over.' A British boy's encounter with Jello includes a whole litany of empirical Americana, from Hershey bars and Dunkin' Donuts to a '200-year-old, 200 foot, triple-masted heavy frigate', the USS Constitution. The truth, said Brecht, is concrete. 'I rehearse the details,' we are told in a text that places a four-year-old on the brink of a deadly fall. 'The rust on the fire escape, the cardboard box.' Those concrete details, like any of the details in serious realist writing, are not only a record of the exterior world; they are a psychograph of the interior world as well. So too, Isaac in the water, his dark hair trailing from his head, 'smooth as a fishtail'. So too, the crocodile taking Uncle Nestor. So too, a horrific accident: 'On the third day of basic the man who sleeps in the bed next to mine loses his fingers when his rifle misfires. I look at him and see him counting time in his head silently as he stares at the blood covering his mutilated hand. As he reaches thirty seconds he opens his mouth and the terror grips him and he falls on his back and flails and writhes on the floor and has to be restrained by two others. But they hold his chest too tight and they don't realise he's having an asthma attack and he dies there, in the training field.' And so too, the knowledge taught by the dark places on this earth: 'Do you know what happens to a home-made time-fused fragmentation grenade when its fuse runs out? Its insides explode, sending out thousands of tiny projectiles at almost incalculable speeds: flechetts, tiny darts that slit the air; notched wire; ball bearings; even the fragments of the casing turn into shards of murder. Within a 15m radius, you're wounded. How bad depends on the grenade. 5m and you're dead.'

So yes, the knowing 'reminds you of the heart of things', as a poem here has it. And that knowing is at once a physical and a metaphysical thing. It is, as another text puts it, a scratch that both fades and doesn't fade. The answer, then, is to write what you know? To that we return a yes, of course, but it has to be a qualified yes. Because where does writing-about-what-you-know leave us when we read sentences like: 'It's always raining down in the archives', or 'Now you've made the alarm clock cry', or 'People are oversleeping in record numbers'? For that matter, how do we get from reading the correspondence of two writers to this? – 'Every letter in the book is an act of nudity. The image that accompanied me as I read the letters was of two young men sitting naked at a small dining table, facing each other with open chests, telling their thoughts out loud. They ignore the desire to sleep. They push through the heavy waves of morning-rationality-regret. When I reached the end of their correspondence I placed the book back on the shelf, and the two young men stood up from the table, dressed and left each other. And that's when my heart broke.' And how, in a text that twines in and out of research into honey-bees, do we arrive at this? – 'His stillness is an encouragement. My heart is fluttering and I can smell honey. The buzzing is getting stronger and moving through my skull. I can just about see his face which I think is smiling, I was right. That tingling in my fingers like hundreds of little legs. Their beautiful bodies squirming now formed from the flesh of my throat.

Yes and my legs could be stems twirling into a beautiful flowering. Now it is hard to move but I think he will come to me, I think he will.'

The stories and poems in this mesmerising collection are well aware of the importance of putting one foot forward, then the next. They walk confidently. They have hit their stride. And it's inspiring to go for a walk with them. But they also know that texts hop, skip and jump, texts dance, texts clasp their limbs to their bodies, texts do whatever they please. 'At the bottom of the estate, in the village of Yasnaya Polyana, the burnt-out husks of cars litter the roadside and families collect rainwater.' Alice walking or in her bath confronts last things not only for herself but for humanity. The blind fisherman is out on the epic waves, trying to draw out Leviathan with a hook. And the story of the writers' correspondence modulates into a grandmother's indignation – a doctor, tossing a coin and challenging children to guess if it comes down heads or tails, doesn't let them see the result, and so could be telling them anything. That can't be right! But then: 'Anything worth inventing in the mind is as true as we care to make it.'

What do we mean by what we know? We mean everything that we know. That includes all of the things we cannot prove, all of the wayward notions that accompany the progress of one-foot-forward-then-the-next, all we have ever imagined or borrowed from others' imaginings. These texts know that. They know how to arrive at dialogue that reads, 'I killed Jane Austen so Allegra could have her in her soup'. They know that the walk, like consciousness itself, may simply go on and on with no full stop until the very end. They are all staged executions, challenging us to imagine what we see when the blindfold comes off. Picture, if you will, Flaubert and Maupassant returned from their own walk. Do they eat sour cream on rye bread toast, or red Jello? How should I know? Do they idly pick up a copy of *Verge*, thumb the pages, start to read, and find it hard to stop? I think they do. 'I'd love to know what you make of it,' says Maupassant to Flaubert, already quoting one of the texts.

JELLO

Jon Mycroft

I WAS BORN in Royal Leamington Spa, a place as English as it sounds. So, for me, America was a strange yet familiar place, half-known from television and cinema. And although I'd never seen much of New England in films or photographs, it felt like New York to me. Of course, when I finally saw Manhattan for myself, I knew better; but to a thirteen-year-old tourist, Boston felt like Vegas and Hollywood all rolled into one. It was America.

Years earlier, my father had become the first transatlantic member of my family; the first of us to make it to the New World and come back with stories and presents and jetlag. The romantic curse of the elite, jetlag was reserved for film stars and pop singers. I was as impressed as I was appalled when I saw my dad, creased and exhausted, dragging his case back over the welcome mat.

When he had finally woken, just before my bedtime, he gave me my exotic gifts. As fantastic as tobacco and potatoes, more lustrous than Aztec gold, I couldn't believe the bounty he had brought for me, his youngest. There were Hershey bars, Nutrageous, Three Musketeers, and a Babe Ruth bar, just like in the Goonies. There were the boxes of Milk Duds I'd seen in Ghostbusters, bags of Lays crisps, or chips I should say, pretzels, jelly beans, bubble gum and more. There were US Opal Fruits called Starburst with different flavours like grape and watermelon. Life Savers, Reese's, Almond Mars, Peanut Snickers, Tropical Skittles, and my absolute favourite, my Star of India: the 5th Avenue bar.

After that heady summer, the memories of candy lingered like a first kiss until years later, at thirteen, when I first crossed the ocean myself in search of confectionary. I spent the flight imagining the mysterious Twinkies, Dunkin' Donuts and Hostess Fruit Pies, all of the things that were advertised in Marvel comics but wouldn't survive the shipping. I would spend hours lying on my bed, engrossed in Spiderman's latest dilemma as he was forced to choose between saving the lovely Gwen Stacy or his kindly Aunt May, then I would greedily turn the page and be suddenly faced with images of cream-filled golden sponge treats, as unavailable and distant as the promised X-ray Specs or Spy-rings. Of all my boyhood dreams and frustrations, Twinkies were high on the list.

And suddenly, there I was, in the heart of modern life, away from fusty Britain with its cold stone museums and hollow churches. Here was the future, happening now. From the moment we landed at Logan International, I wanted to see everything; I wanted to feel it, to hear, smell and taste it. I wanted to taste it most of all. The view from the taxi cab window was enticing. I saw steaming street vents and newspaper boxes. I saw Walk, Don't Walk, and yellow fire hydrants. I was disappointed they weren't red but I'd felt I'd seen something special when the driver told me that they were different in each city. I'd seen something American that normal English people hadn't. As the sound of sirens, more familiar than the ones at home, rang across the city towards me like music I felt ever so slightly expatriated, Americanised.

Boston had the expected feel of America, despite its older architecture. The red brick and bay windows were not what I had imagined, but always above the chimney pots were the skyscrapers of the financial district. I watched the city twinkle from our hotel room window. I could see tiny lights crawling along the stretched silver spider web of Boston Bridge, and it felt like I was in the future.

We spent the morning following the Freedom Trail – a brass line set into the pavements that wound around the city for miles. It snaked past several statues and churches, a graveyard and an old wooden house with leaded windows. It was the house of Paul Revere which, to a boy of my age and interests, was just a place where I had to keep my voice down; a place filled with rather mundane and old fashioned things that I mustn't touch. I was, however, very impressed by the USS Constitution – the 200-year-old, 200 foot, triple-masted heavy frigate. We walked up and down its decks all afternoon, looking at cannons and ropes and sailcloth. I almost completely forgot about the candy.

My father read the guide book entries to me with obvious excitement: Harvard, Franklin Park Zoo, and The JFK Museum. But all I wanted to see was a 7-Eleven. I imagined the flavours, the range, the sheer range! I came from a society with only four channels and two types of Coke. John F. Kennedy be damned, I thought. I wanted Captain Crunch.

By the time we drove out of Boston, towards Cape Cod, I was convinced that I would never taste a Hershey's bar again. I slumped in the back seat in a petulant funk which I dragged all the way to the Plimouth Plantation. Sullen and grumpy, I slouched my way into reproduction homes filled with actors who dressed and behaved like authentic pilgrims. They all had Somerset accents and it started to feel like the holiday was over.

I stumped and kicked at the ground until my mother kept glaring at me. She didn't understand. I'd seen American kids from the West Coast getting dragged around by their parents, but at least they had candy – candy which I suspected they didn't truly appreciate. After the living museum, we found a small diner proclaiming the best chowder in the state. Inside, I scoured the counter for chocolate but there was nothing so I resumed my slouch and slumped into my chair while my parents enjoyed the clams.

I quickly ate my burger and picked at my chips, trying not to breathe the fish-flavoured steam wafting from my parents' bowls. As I reached out idly for the bottle of A1 Steak Sauce, my sleeve caught my glass and I sent fizzy pop all over the gingham tablecloth. We all pressed our napkins into the spreading pool and searched around for more. The blue serviettes drank up the spillage until we were left with a sodden mulch of tissue. My dad gave me a look, so I got up and tried to find a waiter. He was washing a frying pan in the kitchen, I could see him through the doorway; a tall man in spotted chef's whites. He looked up at my cough.

'Sorry, do you have a bin I could use?' I said.

'A what?' he replied, creasing his face in confusion.

'A bin,' I said as clearly as I could.

'A what?' he said again. I started to panic. This was one of those words, one of those double words like sidewalk or pants. He looked at me, his hands on his hips while I searched my mental phrase book: Xerox, subway, couch, diaper. The trunk of the car, the hood of the car. What the hell was it?

'I… I need a receptacle where I can dispose of my refuse…,' I said. It was the best I could manage.

'You mean a trash can?' he said, raising his eyebrows behind his hat-line.

'Yes!' I said, almost jumping. 'Yes, a trash can, for my trash.' I waved the sodden tissue triumphantly.

'It's over here,' he pointed, before walking through to the kitchen, shaking his head gently.

When I got back to the table, my parents were looking at the laminated dessert menu.

'What's Jello?' Mum said. 'Is it a mistake?'

'Jello?' I cried and snatched up a menu. I'd heard of Jello in books or movies. I tried to remember where.

'It's just jelly,' Dad said; but it wasn't, it was Jello, it was different and American. It was new.

'Do they have it?' I said eagerly. 'If they do I'd like to have Jello. Can I?'

'I'm not sure that I want a pudding,' Mum said. I couldn't believe it, not the Jello as well. They couldn't keep waving these delights before me and then snatching them away, this was too much. My dad started to fish around for his wallet and the waiter wandered over.

'Do you have Jello?' I said, ignoring my dad's signal for the bill. He kept on signing the air in imaginary flourishes but I managed to keep the waiter's attention. 'What flavours does it come in?'

'There's red and green, but we're all out of green,' he pulled out his order pad and licked his pencil tip.

'What flavour is red?' I asked. He looked at me.

'It's red flavour. Red fruit,' he said.

'But which fruit? Strawberry? Raspberry?' My head filled with possibilities, with cranberries and pomegranates, with cherries and watermelons, even boysenberry.

'It's red,' he said. 'That's what it's called, Red Jello.'

'Then I'll try some,' I said, and tucked a fresh napkin into my collar.

The gelatinous crimson cylinder soon arrived in a small white bowl. This was to be my first experience of truly American cuisine. I wasn't interested in Philadelphia cheese steak, in clam chowder or Boston beans. I may have missed out on Dunkin' a doughnut but surely this was better, it felt special. After all, a Three Musketeers was just a big Milky Way, and Nutrageous was a lot like Topic. This was real, realer than Real Coke.

I pushed my spoon in carefully, not too far, not to the handle. I levered it back gently, freeing a scoop with a sucking slurp. The quivering lump shone in the strip light. I closed my eyes and savoured the sweet chemical aroma before squelching it softly between my teeth.

'Well?' my father said, 'What's it like?'

'Red,' I said, between pointless chewing, 'it tastes red.'

And it did.

EDDIE IN THE GLOAMING

Rhian Graco

THE SNOW IS fresh today. Fresh and crisp like the sheets Allegra made our bed with. She holds my hand as we walk from the cabin into the village. We take our gloves off so we can feel each other's skin. She smells like lilies.

I call, 'Marco!' and the dog barks back. He's old, but I taught him to answer my call. I can judge how far he is from me.

Flakes catch on my eyelashes; the snow absorbs any sound other than our breathing. I hear cars as we near town, then some blues notes from Dane's guitar shop; I smell raw meat.

Allegra says, 'I saw Ben in the bakery yesterday. He has things to tell you.'

'What things?'

'Important things.'

'That's vague.'

'He said he would be waiting for you at the front of the library and I can see him; he's already there. Do you want me to take you to him while I get the groceries?'

'We're at the butcher now, yes?'

'Yup.'

'I'll find my own way. You get the groceries.'

'Okay, my love,' she lets go of my hand, and kisses me on the cheek. The fur of her collar tickles my neck. The dog will follow her.

Eighteen steps. No cars or pick-ups coming; I can cross.

'Ben?'

'Eddie! I'm on your left, man.'

His voice is a little deeper since I met him last.

'How are you, kid?' I smile at him. I find him and ruffle his hair, just a little. I touch his face, and feel stubble along his jaw. It's been too long.

'Do you wanna go inside, Ed? You cold?'

'No. It's nice out here, don't you think? No wind. It's nice, Ben, nice and calm and clean. Sit on the stairs with me?'

'Okay. I brought you a coffee, by the way, from the corner shop. I forgot how many sugars you have so I got you five.'

I smile. 'Five's just fine.'

He shakes the sachets, and pours the sugar into the coffee with a crackling swoosh. The smell of coffee streaks warmth through me.

'So Allegra says you have news for me.'

'Shit man, you don't muck around do you? Ey? Don't even ask me about my family or anythin', how's school. Jesus.' I can hear the smile in his voice. I touch his mouth, and feel the corners turned toward his eyes. He has full cheeks, deep-set eyes and a strong jaw. He's handsome.

'Alright kid, how's the family? Your mum? Your dad?'

'Good.'

'How's school?'

'Good.'

'Super. Glad we could clarify that. What juicy stuff have you got for me?'

'My driving instructor said to me the other day that the most common mistakes learners make are speeding, and failing to stop,' Ben says with a sort of nervous puff of a laugh.

'You think you're going too fast and you can't stop?'

'Oy, calm down big boy; I don't need you to analyse me just yet.'

He's a fun kid, quick to fire up.

'Just thought I'd avoid the pussy-footin',' I reply.

I hear skin rub skin, like he's rubbing his face with his hands.

'What's wrong, kid? Usually you only want to see me when something's up, so what is it?'

'It makes me feel bad when you say that. That I only see you when I wanna have a whinge about something.'

'All kids need someone to talk to. That someone might as well be me. And I've got all time in the world for you.'

Ben hesitates again.

'Jessie's pregnant. And I,' he stutters a little, 'I dunno what to do about it.' I can hear him rustle in his jacket. I bet he's trying to tuck into it like a turtle.

'You have to do something about it these days?' I joke. I have to lighten the mood or he'll stop talking.

'Don't be a jackass.'

'No, really. What do you have to do when you knock up your girl?'

'I dunno. All I've got so far is to tell her everything is going to be alright. We'll work something out. I was kinda hoping you'd know.'

'Na kid. I was never lucky enough.'

Ben rests his hand near mine. I loop my arm through his. We sit.

'It's a life, Ben. Not a fucking tumour. You don't need to be so terrified.'

He doesn't reply.

'Kid, you'd be surprised how people adapt to things they're not ready for. How they learn along the way. I mean, look at me. The first few months of me being like this, low tables were my worst enemy,' I laugh. 'My shins were black and blue from bumping into everything.'

He shifts his weight. 'Were you scared?' he asks, 'After the accident?'

'I was absolutely fucking terrified, kid. And it might sound daft, but what scared me even more was that Allegra wouldn't stick around. Sure, I'd only dated her for two weeks but they were the best two weeks I could remember.'

'I admire her for staying,' Ben says. 'I'm not sure if I'd be a good enough person to do the same thing.'

'When it first happened we had to have "The Talk",' I say.

'What talk?' Ben asks.

'I told her she should be with someone who can see how beautiful she is and it might be best if we didn't see each other anymore. The whole time I was saying it, I was scared shitless she'd agree and leave me before I'd even finished.'

'How'd she react?' he said.

Remembering her blunt response made me laugh. 'Allegra said: "This isn't a game of goddamn hide-and-seek, Edward. I really like you. I want to keep dating you. So how about you shut down the pity party and ask me about my day?" That was it.'

Ben chuckles. For a few minutes we listen to the town and its humming energy.

I turn my face towards him, 'Everyone assumed me having that accident and going blind was the worst thing that could ever have happened to me. And it's been tough – still is. But there are some things, little moments. Like, how water feels to touch when you can't see it.'

Ben makes a hum of agreement.

I continue, 'And then I heard this quote, by this Spaniard: Spinoza. Something like, "everything great is just as difficult to realise as it is rare to find." It stuck with me. It made me grateful for what I had.'

I hear Ben exhale deeply. He takes a few moments. 'It's too scary, Eddie. I have to try and show this new thing the world and everything. And how to be a good person; how to do things right, you know? I don't even know how to do all that yet, how the fuck am I supposed to show someone else how to do it? I just dunno how we're supposed to do that on our own.'

'Who told you that you were gonna be on your own?'

'No, I mean: it's me and Jessie as parents, and we've never done it before. We don't know what to do. I don't even know how to change a nappy. I'm, I'm fucking scared, man. What if I can't do it right?'

'Kid, look around you. Every person in this town would give their left nut to help you out.' I nudge his shoulder. 'And most of them have parented before and if those skills fail them then, above all, we're good people.'

'I know, mate.'

'Can you imagine how happy it would make this lot? I mean, take Allegra. Having a baby around to take care of? She'd shit herself with glee, Ben.'

This makes him chuckle. 'She would, would she?'

I nod.

'How far in is she?' I ask.

''Bout six weeks.'

'It's got a heartbeat then.'

'Huh?'

'I heard that a foetus has a heartbeat after four weeks.'

'It has a heart?'

'Yeah, kid. And I bet it's as good as yours.' I tap his chest. I feel a wet drop fall on the naked skin between my sleeve and my glove. I take my glove off and feel his face. He shuts his eyes. They are wet. He puts his hands on my face; he does this every time we meet.

'Your beard feels like my pubes,' he says and breaks into hysterical laugher.

'Charming.'

'What are you two love-birds doing?' It's Jessie's voice.

'Hey beautiful,' we say in unison.

She comes to me, and kisses me on the cheek. I stand and we hug. She holds me tighter than usual.

'You'll be a good mum,' I say. She holds me tighter still.

'Allegra said you let Jane Austen die,' she accuses me, pulling out of our embrace.

'You let a chook die?' Ben squeals, sarcastically.

'Hey hang on. Do me a favour and go tell Allegra she's full of shit. I killed Jane Austen so Allegra could have her in her soup, if she remembers.'

Jessie runs across the road. Her boots crunch on the snow.

'What colour did you say your eyes were again?' I ask Ben.

'My eyes?'

'Yes Ben, your eyes. The things you see with.'

'Mum says that my eyes are like the sky. Not that they're blue, but that they change colour depending on the colour of the ocean. When I was real little, I bought into that shit a whole lot easier. Now it just sounds fuckin' ridiculous.'

He makes me laugh.

'You remember what blue looks like, yeah?'

'Yeah. Allegra hangs coloured scarves in the sun-room, so when the afternoon sun hits the windows, it turns into a fucking rainbow. The colours are bright enough for me to see.'

'Maybe we could have scarves. Teach the kids.'

'Maybe we could, Ben.'

We sit. The day darkens, bringing a dampness to the air. I smell my coffee. It has stopped snowing.

Werner Herzog walks from Munich to Paris in an attempt to save his friend's life

Rebecca Tamas

She is sleeping,
her bed dipped in the slow light
of an underwater green.

The moon is sickly pale, malnourished thin.
In the pin drop quiet
patients swallow down their mouths of air.

In the night a tall man walks.
Yes there is ice,
yes the road is long.

Stars prickle, doubt,
(this won't save her)
But blood is something.
It collects in his boots,
soaks through the tip of his socks from the skin.
Currency.
Heat in the thick snow congealing.

Energy cannot be destroyed –
so here in the line of sweat along his lip and tongue
drips energy, pure as star birth.

Who is to stop it making time,
and hope, balanced against his chest like nearly spilling water,
reaching its resting place.

Her breath rises in Paris –
white and small, impossible.

The river is deep and wide.

He goes on.

PREDICTION ON TWELFTH NIGHT

Rebecca Tamas

speckled, fallen

the wind smelling of damp and sea salt

still in the buried husk of January
flesh moves, unravels.

The tea leaves read:

Pack for a journey,
iron your cleanest shirts,
write goodbye notes to unreliable lovers.
You will meet an odd new face
with wide eyes in the mirror.

(Pour the dregs in the sink,
spit for good measure)
You lock the front door, bag in hand –

a flit, a slip, a night flight.

Far above, the northern cross
wheels through the sky in its cold stardom:

which reminds you of the rood and its vision,
which reminds you of the nails and wood and blood,
which reminds you of the sap, the seed, the forest,
the shoot, the thaw, the crack,
    which reminds you of the spreading branches, the ache, the startled
  green;
which reminds you of the heart of things.

CLOUD-WATCHERS

Rebecca Tamas

High Clouds

Cirrocumulus (heaped curl of hair)

Rows and sheets
                shadow free herringbone lacing

                around the curve of cool air

Skin and skein   cold and high

that other side of the pillow chill   which rubs up

                to the vast dark beyond

Cirrus (curl of hair)

Strands,
a mare's tail that
                        flicks the blue
                        wipes the spit from off the cheek.

Fall streaks where it is both fast and slow
A   drag   across

        A wash.

#Middle Clouds

Altostratus (high layered)

A sheet of grey, a breath on the windowpane.
Light is in it
and yet passes through

like
music

underwater.

So frail, a nudge,

so that when you pass a hand over your face   and

feel a   film   of wet
                    so slick, so quiet

you look up
and suddenly realise it's raining.

Altocumulus (high heap)

Sheets and patches
                    the drift of
                              soft
                                        air

Rolling spilt powder over a humid summer morning

with storms in the ante-room.

In the half-light
they
          approach,
dark   and

still

and on the phone someone is reassuring a scared child
that there are no invading aliens

          and nothing to be afraid of.

#Low Clouds

Cumulus humulis (humble heap)

There is a sign.

          How rarely when you can look up

and for once be told

even for a few hours,
that there will be sunshine,
dry hair and warm blankets.
A light aircraft
          swoops in turbulence

with a slide of the stomach
          and the glint of gold off white

that shears the in –
between.

Stratocumulus (bigger heap)

Wide and dark,
a linked and
           pouring heap
over   hot forests
                       and the coldest sea.

Here is dull weather lying like a rope over
horse latitudes

bringing the touch of unease

           where something cools

           and it could go either way.

OH THE DIVORCES

Rebecca Tamas

There is no safety,
put out that match.
Air conditioning provided by the smashed out windows.

But I don't mind saying I like it this way,
I like it.

I think of the maze of soft furnishings in her old house,
I think of her blouses wrapped up in paper packages
and how loud our shoes sounded in the hall.
There are too many to count,
an overflowing vault of drowned, bloated, silent dead.
Skin translucent and invisible.

And you could set fire to it all, and leave me alone in that top attic,
to burn
without a key.

And you would still find me
in a world where I
open the charred door to the air,
and walk.

THE PROCEDURE

Susan Stanford

ALICE HAD CLOSED the window on the screen before she had quite finished reading. Of course, everybody knew that the procedure could affect people in that way. But the fact that it was her first husband – the one who had generally been gentle and considerate – upset her profoundly. She had taken a couple of pills, and had turned on the 4D TV to lose herself in another world. But entirely imaginary images had protruded into her consciousness like fragments of a hologram. The pieces had come together, playing out its seamless horror again and again in her dreams: fourteen people terrified, fourteen people dead before he had put the gun in his mouth, and blew the top off his head.

She woke in pain, cramped, gritty and aching around the heart. The procedure… However much she tried not to think about it, images cascaded in a ghostly apparition at the edge of her mind's eye. There were the ones who had relentlessly stuffed themselves full of gourmet food and died enjoying a last mouthful of truffles; the ones who had starved to mere happy skeletons; the ones who had overdosed; the ones who had taken the route of sex usually combined with various other thrills; those who had run, swum out to sea; those who had chosen mediation; those who had worked themselves to death. Murder, especially mass murder, was less and less usual. After all, anyone could safely partake of that release through a great number of multisensory games.

It was a pleasure to take a bath. Alice lay back in the hot water and thoughtlessly allowed the tip of her tongue to wander against the inside of one cheek. A roughness surprised her. Wounds. There was a long welt on the other side too. In the privacy of sleep her teeth had left the marks of her otherwise inaccessible life.

Apart from Nobuko, she was alone, now. No one would be troubled by whether she decided this way or that. Was it worth persevering with this difficult daily struggle, when you could be rid of fear? People made this decision every day.

Alice felt the powerful pleasure of her blood surging through her body. She listened to the marvellous jangling of the magpies in the garden. She breathed in the steamy air, letting her edges dissolve. Her dreams, her shock, floated away.

Now she was free to let her mind wander. Images from her library of wordless picture-books replayed themselves, unfixed and absent at the same time. She liked *The Elephant's Buttons* the best. She tried to remember the order of every page, visualising each smaller cloth animal emerging from the unbuttoned belly of the one before. Then on the large page she saw how from the mouse came one more enormous elephant. It was reassuring to think that the cycle always starts again.

She soaped herself. Soaped deep into her ears and between her toes. And then slipped, luxuriously under the hot water.

Even at her age her body was strong. The brutal strength of its desire to live reinforced the knowledge that her distant ancestors had held out stubbornly when other creatures had carelessly fallen asleep in the snow, or had too willingly given themselves up to be eaten. Fear was the bass line in the choir of this strong body – this body that did not want to die.

The birds were plentiful. There were magpies around her patch. Blue wrens, bellbirds, willy wagtails – all sorts of old acquaintances were returning. The primal forests of Chernobyl and Fukushima had been quite a lesson. Even radioactivity will do it. If something keeps humans at bay the earth renews itself.

She walked her normal route, under the rampant tree tunnels, past the large decaying suburban houses. Every season brought more wildlife. In her basket she carried freshly baked bread and a casserole to eat with Nobuko. Unlike Red Riding Hood, she'd checked her screen for packs of wild dogs before she left. The screen told her there were many further out, but they were still rare in Malvern. Her errand was not urgent. This kitchen fiddling, this tasting, arranging, this whole exchange of dishes was merely a pastime. The bots made them personally adjusted perfectly balanced meals. Her food was not as optimal as theirs. But if she gave up cooking too, how would she organise her day?

Nobuko's bot, Jessica, checked her profile and welcomed her into the house. Nobuko was watching the Uplifting News.

'I'll turn it off. I know you hate it! I don't know why I've got it on, myself.'

'I made some bread and spicy beans. I thought it would be nice to have a chat.'

Jessica laid out the meal, and joined them to play a few hands of abec.

The chat was desultory at first. Alice said nothing about what had appeared the evening before on her screen. Then Nobuko took a deep breath. She'd decided to fly to Florida and see her grandchildren and then she'd check herself in.

'I'm ready. I'm not sure what I'll do next. But I've decided to have the procedure done.'

Alice nodded, half-involuntarily grasping her left hand with her right, to cover her mood ring. She knew at once that Nobuku had noticed the gesture, and was aware that she was hiding her emotion. But she didn't want to disclose a feeling that she could not quite resolve herself. She loved her friend and didn't want to lose her. Didn't want to stop her. Didn't want to argue. She didn't want to make her own decision on the basis of Nobuko's. Not without further thought at least. She was afraid to talk about her news or her own churning irresolution.

Since the procedure had become available at minimal cost, it had cast a long shadow. Alice looked at Nobuko's long oval face with a sudden objectivity. Her eyes glowed almost flat against her still smooth skin. Her tiny chin and the unusual length of her cheeks make it look as though her large wide mouth, a casualty of gravity, had slid slightly out of place. It was a self-contained face. Nobuko was so disciplined and calm it didn't strike you that she was afraid of death. But to be afraid of death, and to struggle to overcome that fear, both of these things, were profoundly human.

The procedure had only been used in hospices at first. It modified the instinctual make up, completely extinguishing the fear of death. People coped better with pain. They had no anxiety. Many had died smiling.

Initially, the protocols had been stringent – but people always found a way to get what they wanted. Obviously the rich and famous had been first in line. An underground industry sprang up. Sports people got hold of it. Hanggliders. Scuba-divers. Proselytising visionaries and virtual reality wizards.

Then suddenly it seemed the perfect answer to over-population. Almost anyone who wanted to enhance their sense of power and freedom booked themselves in. The procedure, once daring and cutting-edge, became commonplace. It didn't always lead to suicide or sudden death, but that was the general pattern. A few continued to live for many years, but eventually most gave up before their time. Or perhaps they'd already given up when they chose to have the procedure done? Offering herself to help the feral children appealed the most to Alice. Too risky to try it if you cared about your own skin. But by now there were very few to help. The procedure had become available even to them.

With a quick shake of her head, Alice got up and hugged her friend. Held and released the warm and transient body of another human being. They would meet again.

It was a pleasure to take a bath. Alice lay back in the hot water and closed her eyes. She knew she would be more than welcome to make her appointment and have it done with Nobuko. She knew Nobuko would never ask. Pain gripped her as she thought about the feral children. Magpies were conversing in the garden. The birds and the bots would inherit this lovely, lovely earth.

THE LAKE

Nkandu Chipale Mwenge

BWACHA, AN INSIGNIFICANT village in Lubwe, was my home. The compound I lived in faced Lake Chifunabuli. From the veranda of my hut, I could see the reeds swaying to the Lake's current; fishermen's canoes were staked to iron rings on the shore, and fish eagles soared over its surface.

The compound was owned by my grandparents; my parents were studying in Lusaka at the time. There were four buildings in the compound. My grandparents lived in the main house, which was the only building with a corrugated-iron roof – the other buildings were thatched. I occupied one with my three young cousins; their parents – Uncle Chali and Aunty Makungu – lived in another, while Uncle Nestor had one to himself.

I come from a family of fishermen: my ancestors fished in Chifunabuli. Some are said to have died in the Lake, while others caught fish so large they became legend. Uncle Nestor was the only family member who continued the trade.

I never wanted to become a fisherman despite the girls at play always saying they wanted to marry one. They said fishermen have big hands and bring home lots of meat. But I didn't see what the girls saw; fishermen have disproportionate bodies, big shoulders, big arms and scrawny legs. And they stink.

I had a change of heart about fishing when Mulenga told me she preferred fish over caterpillars. Mulenga was the first girl I had feelings for. She had short kinky hair, skin as black as fertile soil and a wide waist. I spent many afternoons watching her sway her hips in the Kalela dance troupe.

I started fishing when I was thirteen. As I waited to enter secondary school, I became Uncle Nestor's only crew member in his *mukwa* canoe.

'My boy,' Uncle Nestor said each time he was about to tell me a story on the Lake, 'let me tell you about my expeditions to the bottom of Lake Chifunabuli. When I was a boy like you, your father and I would swim in the Lake naked.

'On one fateful day, we were swimming far out near where we are tonight. I saw a beautiful fish-woman dressed as sinfully as we were. I swam to her as any young man would. When I got to her, she told me her name was Mary and asked if I wanted to go to the bottom of the Lake with her. I agreed.

'She took me to the bottom of these waters where no clean soul can go. When I ran out of breath, she breathed into my mouth; that's how I kept alive, if you're wondering. I never knew how long I spent with her; sunlight doesn't reach the bottom of the Lake so I couldn't tell day from night. When I returned home, they had already held a funeral for me. Your dumb father said a crocodile had eaten me. You're lucky I'm bringing you up otherwise you would be a stupid idiot like him.' Uncle Nestor laughed before taking a swig of the local wine he had brought with him.

'What was it like at the bottom, Uncle?' I asked.

'It is a beautiful place, gold and rubies make up the floor. A queen fish-woman rules over the creatures of the Lake; there are monsters I cannot describe and men who turn into crocodiles, menacing creatures. They nibbled on me when they were hungry; they must have been jealous because I had taken one of the most beautiful fish-women and she and I had agreed to marry. You find all kinds of food there, food reserved for gods. Every day was a feast.

'The queen fish-woman summoned me to explain the traditions of the underwater beings. She said I was to marry Mary and live there for eternity, never to see dry land again. I had to leave. I couldn't live for eternity and never smell soil after a rainy day or feel the warmth of the sun. I liked Mary, maybe even loved her, and no walking woman could match her beauty. But imagine never dying, never growing old, never wrinkling, never having to reconstruct truths about one's past adventures.' Uncle Nestor paused, smiled dryly and his eyes lingered on me. 'I couldn't, and still can't imagine not doing any of these things, so I left.'

'But Uncle, if there was lots of food, why did the men who turned into crocodiles want to eat you?' I asked him.

'You ask too many irrelevant questions, young man. It happened as I have told you.'

Sleeping in the canoe was unpleasant on the first few nights. I lay in the splintered hull thinking of the men who turn to crocodiles and beautiful fish-tailed women taking fishermen to the depths of the Lake. I quaked in my skin. As I spent more nights on the Lake, I grew accustomed to the waves rocking me to and fro as a mother does a baby. The wind that had once sounded like dead men howling sung me lullabies and Uncle Nestor's snoring reminded me that I was alive.

Sometimes I dreamt Mulenga was the fish-woman in Uncle Nestor's stories, the waves caressing her dark skin, her breath keeping me alive and our love enduring for eternity. I decided I would live for eternity if Mulenga would be my partner.

'Chabu,' Uncle Nestor shook me awake before sunrise, 'It is time to tow the net.'

We cast the nets at night and attracted fish with fluorescent lamps, then towed the net before dawn to avoid the fish scattering in the sunlight. It was a brutal time: the cold wind cut our skin and sometimes almost threw us overboard. The waves came at us from all sides. On some days, the current was so strong the rope snapped and we returned home hungry, tired and with no fish.

My cousins would welcome us at the compound expecting fish. If Uncle Nestor and I had caught nothing, we would head to our huts to sleep. The children never asked if we had fish with us. They saw the empty nets and had to return to their *nshima*, made from cassava tubers, and *katapa* – pounded cassava leaves. From my hut, I sometimes heard my youngest cousin crying for fish. Aunty Makungu would hush him with warnings of a beating.

'Stop crying now!' she would say.

'But I'm hungry,' he replied.

'Shut up, the gods were not with your elders today. You will have fish tomorrow.'

'I don't want *katapa*. Every day we have *katapa*,' my cousin would sob. How regularly a family ate *katapa* was the measure of how poor they were.

'Stop crying or I am going to beat you. Shut up.' There would be a slap and more crying. At those moments my hunger went away, my exhaustion faded and the dreams of Mulenga became less enjoyable. I lay on my mat and imagined how many bellies were rumbling because I hadn't returned with fish.

On some days, we returned home with a big catch and Aunty Makungu took the surplus to market. Our market stand faced the Kalela dance ring, where Mulenga practised every day before sunset with the village's dance troupe. In the midst of the beating drums and dust, she would emerge swaying her hips. I ululated to cheer her on and Aunty Makungu twisted my ear. 'Ey! Don't you know boys don't ululate?' she scorned me. I hated her as she ululated and shouted, 'Ah Mulenga, the pride of the village.' And I hated her husband, Uncle Chali, who spent whatever we earned at The House of the Rising Sun. He never fished because of a bad hand. But his hands were never bad when he got into fights.

When I wasn't fishing, I spent my mornings like every child in the village: in the bush. We would pick caterpillars from tree leaves, *masukus* that had fallen to the ground, hunt for mushrooms, and swim in the stream or play hide and seek.

It was one of the few times I got to play with Mulenga. We were playing hide and seek and Mulenga was looking for a place to hide. I called out to her from the shrub I was hiding behind and gestured that she should hide with me. She came over in a rush. 'Do you think we will be found here?' she asked.

'No, it's safe here.'

Her blouse was a clumsy fit for her and I could see her breasts pointing through it. Her breast knobs were unlike the wrinkled breast knobs of Aunty Makungu, they looked hard and strong. I felt the urge to touch them. I reached towards her and she slapped my hand away. 'Ey, what's your problem?' she said.

'I'm sorry, I didn't mean to.'

'The only time you can touch my breasts is when we play house and only if I choose you to play husband.'

'But you choose me to play the dog all the time,' I replied.

'You never asked to play the father.'

'Can I just touch them now? Please?' I felt my jojo stir; it hardened and I had to find a way to hide it. I didn't want Mulenga to see it big; it was embarrassing and would scare her away.

'No, you can't,' she said.

My jojo was big now and I ran to another bush to hide it.

The next time I was with Uncle Nestor, he was listening to his audio cassette player. He was happiest when he was listening to his compilation of Willie Dixon, Bob Marley and Kool and the Gang. I asked him, 'Uncle, what am I supposed to do when my jojo is big?'

Uncle Nestor gave a quick grin. 'Why do you ask, my boy?'

'I was with Mulenga the other day and my jojo became hard. I was afraid it would scare her so I ran away.'

'You're still young, boy,' Uncle Nestor said, 'Next time run to the well and pour water on it.'

'Is that all?' I asked.

'Do that and it will all go away.'

I sat with Uncle while he listened and sang along to his music.

One evening Uncle Nestor told me we were going fishing. The clouds where thick and black, and the waves were higher than usual. When we got to the Lake, no one was fishing that night; no one was brave or stubborn enough.

'Uncle Nestor, isn't it dangerous to fish tonight?' I asked, hoping to dissuade him.

'Boy, when will you realise your Uncle is a god? Come on, let's go.' He tugged me by the arm. 'We will not cast the net far,' he said, pushing the canoe into the Lake. 'We will stay near the shore; don't worry.'

When we were just beyond the reeds, Uncle Nestor asked, 'How is Mulenga?'

'I don't know,' I replied.

'Okay, you don't want to talk to your favorite uncle now.'

I laughed, 'Uncle Chali is my favorite uncle. I want to be just like him, spend my nights at The House of the Rising Sun.'

'Oh, and have an ugly wife like him, too?'

'I'm not allowed to talk about my elders like that.'

Uncle Nestor told me he had had a fight with Uncle Chali, a fight he didn't want to talk about. Then he recounted a tale about his expeditions on the Lake, about the time he fought a gruesome monster. I don't know when or how I slept in the turbulent weather; we talked long into the night.

'Chabu,' Uncle Nestor shook me early in the morning, 'Wake up, we have to tow the net now; it's too windy to stay on board.' It was overcast and the waves were even higher than when we set out.

I flipped my blanket and took a piss in the water before I untied the rope that connected the net to the canoe. The current was strong against the net, and it almost tugged me into the water. The canoe tilted to one side and then the other. I wobbled, trying to regain my balance. Uncle Nestor was struggling to pull in the net when the rope snapped and he fell backwards into the water. As he surfaced, he tried to swim back to the canoe but something took hold of him and pulled him under the waves.

I just stood in the canoe, not knowing what to do. Uncle Nestor's head and shoulders emerged from the water; he made a grasp for the boat but was too far out. There was blood all around him.

Then I saw the monster, the crocodile nose followed by a tail flipping like a small wave. In one swift movement, the crocodile drilled its teeth into Uncle Nestor's collarbone with a crack. It shook him; his head tilted to the side and he made no effort to fight the creature. Blood gushed out of his neck, blood so thick it frothed the water around him.

I steered the canoe towards him, but the crocodile pulled him under before I could get there. I followed the trail of blood. Wind blew hard against the canoe as I searched the water and waves spilled over the sides. The blood trail thinned as the water mixed with it. I dared not jump in; I just waited in the canoe, recalling the times I spent with my uncle.

I sat in the canoe deciding it would be the last time I would ever be on Lake Chifunabuli. I would leave for Lusaka; not even Mulenga's affection would be enough to make me stay.

I'M STILL HERE

Cameron Dick

I STAND ON the edge of the fire escape, the shoulder straps of my small cardboard box plane digging into my skin. I am four – too young for nostalgia, too young even for memory. Each moment is an extended part of the present. It is a dreaming of an existence so fragile that when at last the gears of my adolescence catch and grind forward, it will disperse as though I never in fact stood here, my small hand gripping the rusted iron with the wind behind me, nestling against the cereal box wings of my plane.

*

'Do you know what will happen if you fall?' my brother calls.

His voice is faint from the bottom of the tree, but I am content to ignore the warning as a trick of the wind. I am seven, almost eight, and the rough hide of the pine tree rubs against my palm. Each hand is an anchor and I cast off from it, swinging up to the next branch – always the next branch, my skin becoming scratched and torn like tissue paper.

'I'm going to go get Mum,' he yells, and this time the warning is slightly more real and it reaches and turns me inside out. At once I grow heavier in the tree and the sap burns in the cuts in my hand, and the bark begins to slide where once it stood firm beneath my shoes. The tree sways and in my limited way I realise that I am a fool and begin to sense how inhospitable so much of the world is. I *can* fall and in that insight I am not so much afraid of the fall, but of the existence of falling. I begin to cry and far below I watch my brother run off in the direction of our house. I will not call for help though. I make myself this promise, and I won't go back on my word.

*

'Your luck will run out, you know,' my father says to me. 'God's miracle, wasted.' I can tell he wants to look at me – wants to take his eyes off the dark road and let his gaze rest on me until I feel uncomfortable and his message strikes home. But I am thirteen and I no longer fall for theatrics – I am no longer sensitive to the way silence tries to sneak guilt under a closed door in a conversation. I sit there soaking wet in the passenger's seat, the water bleeding darkly into the fabric. For a moment I experience a rush of self-pity, as if the universe has arbitrarily chosen me as its victim.

'You knew they were opening the reservoir,' he begins and his voice breaks. 'Dammit,' he says, wiping his eyes quickly before returning his hand to the wheel.

Silence intrudes but I cannot enjoy it, knowing that any second it will be broken. I anticipate the intrusion of his voice, and so the silence is spent waiting for the sound.

'Is it that you want to…?' he says and in the darkness of the car it seems as though he's cast a spell. The car's velvety shadows become gloomy; the air humid with an excess of his heavy breathing. I press my head against the window and am not so much ashamed as embarrassed. What he wants to say is something deep and intimate. Something as meaningful as love; but as perverse as saying *pussy*. Something a school boy says jokingly, but in saying it immediately goes red in the face.

'… die,' my father says at last and I hate him for his betrayal, his ignorance. He says the word like an accusation, and I cringe as his tongue touches the word that has been mine from the beginning.

'Do you remember when you were four?' he asks me, and I press my forehead harder against the windowpane. He can never understand, can never grasp the emptiness of having such a deep certainty betrayed. Something that should have been forgotten but that has been countlessly revisited at each family reunion, at each wrongdoing. The same conclusion drawn from the same dream – *you shouldn't be here.* Yet I am, having stolen my life back.

How can I take them at their word? I was there, I remind myself again and again. I rehearse the details. The rust on the fire escape, the cardboard box. The sudden gust of wind.

*

I stand on the edge of the fire escape, the shoulder straps of my small cardboard box plane digging into my skin. I am four – too young for nostalgia, too young even for memory, but it doesn't matter. Even if I cannot remember, I will be instructed in the way that it happened. The storytelling will become my embellished identity; a landmark that I cannot lose in the curve of the world.

The back door is open. It should have been locked, but for some reason that day it wasn't. Let's call it fate.

But I have nothing to fear, for I am still ripe for the miracle – still worthy... *And He will command his angels concerning you...* If I remember anything at all about that moment, I remember looking down from the seventh floor and even from a distance, the pavement seemed cold and uninviting... *They will lift you up in their hands...* The push, the sudden weightlessness... *So that you will not strike your foot against a stone...* A gust of wind. Then flight.

A Staged Execution

Zoë McMinn

1.

If you die blindfolded you can choose to   imagine
you're dying in a field beside
soldiers the way it should be when a Captain or a Corporal
becomes a corpse and

if you die blindfolded you can choose to imagine that you're dying in a
field
beside a   girl.
With her it's like your throat has
come to life and trailed   out
in ravels of red hair to lay beside you propped on her elbow.
A cloud seems to be perched on her shoulder with
skin that smells of   sun-cream and
with your face to the sun
        through your warm eyelids
you see a colour that is at once a complete and solid red
and an amber and a ludicrous shade of yellow.
Your eyes are shut
but you hear her smile
in the change of the rhythm   of her breathing.

If you die blindfolded you can choose
to imagine you're dying in a field beside yourself   with the sightlessness
completing the silence that comes right before the   click
of a trigger   and the blindfold
      becomes a cocoon; like
      how it feels when
      love is so certain it's a tent around you
         or a smell   like sun-cream.

2.

And actually on
the other side of the blindfold you're in a dark room
      surrounded by a huddle of armed   men
      all looking   at you.
You recall them from behind your eyes as   sprawled
two dimensional   like a city
viewed from space. Then

Someone in that armed gaggle
drops
         something that sounds like
a penny.
You hear it   precisely and you wonder who   dropped it and
how many will see it.
    before one man, thirty-one, bearded, looks down and sees the
coin and thinks of the appropriate lucky rhyme
and weighs it up with the memory
of the smell of copper on his hands after handling small change then
      he looks to this person
blindfolded   tied to a chair

He watches
	a sweat-drop
a shake   the constant quake of chin
sees how the clenched jaw tenses	the temple where a	cool
9mm
    P226
        SIG
            Pistol
waits
	He hears this blindfolded person breathing	unsteady
in a ready/not-ready-for-death tense and
he even thinks he sees a	smile beneath the blindfold
	as if to find this all a joke
		all unreal like the	blindfold is unreal;
		a fold of	artificial blindness.
And as you wait for your death you think	you can't decide
which one of those fields	you'd rather die in
	and you try to pick
	as you wait for the sound of the click
	of a trigger.

Then the man scoops up the penny and he thanks	every penny he's
ever picked up that
he's not	blindfolded and tied to a chair
	waiting
for the sound of the click of a trigger
then
a loud click and a faltered gasp—ha—
as a 200watt bulb flicks on and shoots out	light.
	Everyone	relaxes

The gun is not fired, but
in that moment you chose   the field
you were going to die in and
the bearded man will never   know which one you chose

3.
all point and no bullet
      he wonders if there is much difference to you.

Epilogue
then he spots that a beam of light
has made a direct hit on your blindfold
         and wonders if   in your practice-death
you might've felt warmth
on your eyelids and seen all at once
red and amber and yellow and thought
      it was the sun.

ISAAC

Anna Lea

I'M AWAKE BEFORE Isaac. My head's pounding and the room swims about a little when I blink. By all rights, I shouldn't have to see the world again until midday. But it's my brother that sleeps on silently, oblivious to the dawn and the birds that have woken me. When he wakes, his eyes will focus perfectly, intent on his next goal: beating me in our first race of the year. I can see the river from our window. There's a slow current that pushes the water into little peaks. It's catching the light like a sheet of battered tin.

I sneak outside for a smoke and a coffee. That usually sets me right. There's a mist coming off the river now like it's a hot bath. It'll be freezing though. It's only April and I'm starting to shiver just standing here. Birds are sitting in the trees and on the phone line. They make so much noise and at this time, before anyone's up, it's like they own the world.

A hand grabs my shoulder. I spin round.

'Morning.'

It's Isaac.

'Jesus, you scared the life out of me.'

'Ready to swim then?'

We head down to the mooring and strip down to our trunks. The cool air makes us shiver, so we warm up. For me, this means a few quick stretches to get my blood going. But Isaac must put his athletic body through a full set of precise moves. It's a blend of preparation and showing off. He straightens up now and looks at me.

'Set? Go.'

We launch off in unison. The water is so cold it knocks the breath out of me and makes the world sharp, like cut glass. I dive further out than Isaac and I'm ahead for a few strokes. But Isaac has perfected his crawl, and he's overtaking me already. His face is like a ghost, flashing out of the water with every turn of his body. My limbs are going stiff as I try to catch up with him. I haven't been in the water since the end of summer last year – I'm a dead weight to myself.

Isaac pushes through the freezing water, slick as an eel. His body is almost silver as he slips beneath the surface for the final stretch. The trail of bubbles behind him disappears as he sinks out of sight.

I speed up to reach the far side without an embarrassing length between us and feel a tightening in my chest. I block out the cold and the pain and focus on the buoy that hangs from the concrete bank ahead of me. Reaching it, I grab onto the rope that hangs at its side. I take a deep breath and wipe my eyes. I look around, but I can't see Isaac anywhere. I'm waiting for him to break through the surface, ask what took me so long. Nothing.

He does this. He's always done this. Disappear, make us all think he's had it, then appear again out of nowhere to remind us of his brilliance and how much we all love him. He quotes from one of his favourite Westerns: *thought I was a goner, eh?... Should've known ya can't get rid a me that easy.* He tips up his hat, spits out the juice from his chewing tobacco.

When Isaac was really young, he seemed to like me. He'd play whatever game I wanted and I'd get the best roles; the cowboy, the astronaut, the pilot. Then he started making his own games and his own rules. But I was seven by then and I had my own friends. I didn't need him. He soon found other friends, who stayed loyal to him for years, until we moved. Then he found more friends to trail after him. I know how they feel sometimes, because Isaac always gets what he wants. The world is in his control, so you don't have to worry so much. I'd never tell him that, of course.

I hold onto the rope with both hands now and let my body hang into the water. Something slips by my feet – the tail of a fish or the leaf of a plant. I look down, but I can only see just below the surface of the murky water. The shape of my hips and the top of my legs disappear into nothing. I think about last night. I got home late, pissed and ecstatic from seeing Catherine. Isaac had made an excuse for me again and only turned briefly in his bed when I finally came home.

'Fun?' he'd asked.

'Mm hm.'

'Good. I said you were at Mark's doing maths. You were going to stay for dinner and get dropped off by his parents.'

Isaac's dull voice managed to accuse me through the darkness. I heard him pick up the glass of water he always kept beside his bed and take a mouthful before putting his head to the pillow again.

'Thanks,' I said. 'Swim in the morning, yeah?'

'If you're up to it,' his voice was muffled by the pillow.

'Course I am.'

I should have seen it coming, his stylish, effortless victory. I'm still waiting for him. I look across the river, follow the path that we swam. Nothing. Not a single disturbance or trace of where we had been. On the far bank, the trees are swaying in the breeze and I can glimpse the roof of our house.

I scan the water all around me and off to the left where there's a tiny island in the middle of the river. We used to play there when we were younger, when it seemed vast. The island has its own little bay where the water shallows and laps against the muddy shore. There's no sign of Isaac anywhere, so I shout out to him.

'Isaac? Isaac?… Come on, stop messing about. You know you've won.'

It's been at least a minute now. He's under the water somewhere, waiting for the right moment to spring up on me. I swim over to the bay and squint my eyes to scan beneath the water. I can feel my heart beating fast and hard. Now that I've stopped swimming, I'm freezing cold and I can't quite focus on things. I want to get out and back to the house to get warm.

'Isaac, I'm freezing my balls off, come on.'

I expect him to break through the water like a shark, lunging and wide-mouthed. As the water shallows, I see a flicker of something half-hidden. Part of it brushes against my foot, swaying with the tide I've made. It's a half-rotten branch. I kick it and it lolls there, gently rocking, then brings something bobbing up to the surface. A pale, bluish hand. Isaac.

I see the dark hair trailing from his head. The water makes it smooth as a fishtail. There is a second here, free of panic. I'm just looking at my brother beneath the water. Then part of me wants to swim away – pound through the water and lose him. Stand on the bank with my mum and watch someone else drag him out of the water. Him, or his body. Is he dead?

I shout his name, but he doesn't move. I reach for the ground with my feet until the water comes up to my neck. I stand on tiptoe. I reach again to pull him by the shoulders, but from this angle I have no strength. I draw a breath and push myself down beneath the water, grab him under his armpits. They're still warm. He's still warm. I pull as hard as I can. My feet slip and I crash down, swallowing water and quickly choking. I surface for a second and catch a glimpse of Isaac's glassy, lifeless eyes. There's a part of me that suddenly aches with fear. I let out a garbled scream and cough up the last of the water I had swallowed. I'm shivering, my teeth are clattering together and I'm just trying to keep it together. I've got to be sharp. Focused.

I draw breath again and dive underwater. I force my eyes open and see one of Isaac's legs floating free, the other caught in some plastic mesh half-buried in the riverbed. I swim down towards him and tug at the plastic. It's twisted tight around his foot. I stretch it and try to push his foot back out, but it's too tight. I tug on a single length of plastic until it thins and finally snaps. Isaac floats free. I swim back up to the surface and grab him under his arms, gasping to get air back in my lungs.

Isaac's face is not his own. His mouth sags and the river water is spilling out, leaving a faint green trail across his chin. I haul him up as far as I can onto the bank and try to remember what I'm supposed to do. There are always things you're meant to do at times like this. My head is at his chest before I even begin to think. Is that him, or my own blood beating against my ears? Listen – closer – is that a faint beat? I turn him onto his side and slap his back, trying to get the water out.

He coughs without trying and water spurts out of his mouth. Then he's still again.

'Isaac? Isaac!'

I pull him up closer to me, hold him tight as if I can let life seep into him. He doesn't move. I let his body flop onto the bank, then heave him up further so he can't slip back in. I know there are nettles here – I don't take time to avoid them. As I stumble back into the water, I don't even look back at him. I swim, fast as I can, but I'm panicked and spluttering. I pull myself up onto the mooring and run to the house.

I wake Mum and Dad with my screaming. I tell them what's happened and I think maybe that will be enough to undo it all. But it's only making it worse. I'm standing at the edge of their bed – dripping wet – and I start to cry. I can't remember the last time I cried in front of them. I'm imagining Isaac and the nettle stings blooming on his skin.

*

We follow the ambulance to the hospital. We don't speak and every sound is louder than usual. The indicator switch, the windscreen wipers, the engine ticking over at the lights. I count the lamp posts as we pass them. There are enough of them that other thoughts can't creep in. I draw a shape on the misted glass with my finger and think about the ambulance. It is the safest looking thing I've ever seen – neat, important, prepared. That's what the stickered lettering and fluorescent stripes said: we know what's happening and we've got it under control.

Now we're at the hospital, there's nothing to distract me. We sit in a waiting room with a few other people who are bored, or asleep. The tables are covered in glossy magazines for women and the floor is covered in toys. Nurses walk in and out of rooms, folders cradled in their arms, pills in little cups held steady on a tray. It's raining outside – I can hear the rattle of it on the roof. I'm tired, and I ache like I'm about to get the flu or something.

A young nurse pushes an empty wheelchair down the corridor, her eyes fixed on the cushion and blanket left crumpled in the seat. She feels me watching her and her eyes flick up to meet mine. They are a deep, unfiltered blue. I feel a shiver of attraction run through me and a deep regret echoing straight after. My mind makes the quick link to Catherine, but I don't let it wander further than the curve of her neck.

Dad sits next to me, one arm curled around Mum's back, the other gripping his own knee to steady himself. They haven't said a word to me and I've avoided looking at them. I wonder if they know that I was out last night. That I made sure Isaac would race me. I buy them tea from the vending machine with the change I earned from my paper round. I choose the button that says milk and sugar, because that's what you're supposed to give people in shock. Sweet tea.

There's a fat little kid sitting on the floor near our feet now. He's banging a plastic tambourine on the floor and the sound is making Mum upset, I can tell. She's not looking at the kid, just swapping her cup of tea from one hand to the other when it gets too hot to hold. I bend down and smile at the kid who looks up at me, then opens and closes his mouth like a fish. I grab a fluffy monkey that's lying nearby, bounce it up and down in front of him then slip the tambourine out of his hands. Now he's holding the monkey and sucking on its ear.

I walk outside to join the crowd of smokers huddled under the canopy to the side of the main entrance. I beg a roll-up from a guy about my age and he lets me smoke it in silence.

When I walk back in, Mum and Dad are talking to a doctor further down the corridor. They nod in agreement at what the doctor has just said and start to move off. Only Mum pauses to see if I'm back. She waves for me to join them. I run the distance between us and she holds my hand by gripping her fingers around mine, the way she did when I was little.

We walk into Isaac's room and stand around his bed. I look down at him, but focus only on the white sheet and the shape of his body under it. The doctor talks to us across the bed. He says words that mean nothing to me. Mum's already crying. The doctor picks up a clipboard from the bedside and keeps talking. Eventually, his mouth is moving and no sound is coming out.

INSIDE MY HEAD

Georgia Townley

HAVE YOU EVER wondered what goes on inside your head? Have you thought that wondering about it is something that goes on inside your head? I bet you haven't, I bet you don't even think about it, don't worry about it, why would you when you can't know, no one can, except me, I've found out, that's right, I've found out and maybe I could share it with you, you don't have to listen, most people don't, not in here, not now, but I don't care, so come in close if you want, I have the time, I could tell you all day, if you also had the time, but most people don't, not a problem though, I still have the time, I should probably start by introducing myself, I am, well I guess I was, no I probably still am, I'm, well, I'm here and I have a secret, a secret that is not meant to be spoken of, not to anyone, not a single soul, at least, no one has actually told me to keep it to myself, so maybe it isn't a secret, not like most secrets anyway, more of a fact, a fact that no one knows, I'm telling you I'm the only one, and it's that type of knowing when you're totally sure of something, because you found out the hard way, well not hard, maybe just suddenly, or like something that happens when someone shouts 'Hey watch out for th...' then bam a ball smacks you in the head, ha, yeah it's exactly like that, well it happened in my head anyway, but there was no one to shout, not even that silly half sentence, because let's face it, it doesn't work, might as well not say anything at all because the half sentence only makes people look over, then bam, they've turned the exact direction of that flying ball, right into their face, I didn't understand what happened when it first hit, but now I do, it took me a while but through all this calmness, if calmness is the word, through it all I discovered why I was hit by that ball, well a metaphorical ball, that's right I can use big words, I'm not stupid, I went to school, of course I did, everyone does, so I learnt that fancy word that means that something is something else, but you don't want to be obvious about it, because if everyone was so obvious then there'd be no excitement, there certainly wouldn't be any secrets, they would freely float around like candy floss, yes that's a simile, I learnt that around the time of metaphors, I find similes easier though, anything can be like anything else, well an elephant can't be like a lion, unless he was really, really angry or something, or sneaky, I wonder if lions are really sneaky or if we just think they are, maybe no one else thinks that, maybe I'm thinking of foxes, like the one that ate our rabbit, Margret, don't laugh at the name, I chose it, I thought it was fitting, Margret was so quiet and independent, I thought the name would suit, like my Aunt Margret, she died, maybe that's why I called the bunny Margret, yes that's probably why, that was a long time ago, I must have been here a long time now, I think too long, they say just a little longer, so I sit and wait for them to admit that I'm right and it's time to go, but during my long time here, what I realised is that, I'm not making this up now, I don't exactly have proof, but I know, you know when you just know, well that's me, Miss Know, ha, so bear with me, if it seems crazy, I shouldn't use that word, not in here, my apologies, so you see me speaking and you hear the words and then in your head you go, oh yeah, I know what she means, well that doesn't just happen by magic, not like abracadabra, then bam, rabbit in a hat, Margret never liked to do that, no not like magic, I realised there's actually little people, I mean tiny, smaller than you can see so you'll never see them anyway, they can't leave your head, it's not like some kind of motel where you go in just for one night and then leave in the morning and don't look back, no you never ever look back, they can't leave, I almost feel sorry for them, they are trapped in there, I feel empathy for them, another word I can use, it's like sympathy, but it means you've been in their shoes, well not their actual shoes, because, like I said, they are tiny, teeny tiny, their shoes wouldn't fit a mouse, well a mouse-sized human, or just something with tiny feet, I'm not even completely sure they wear shoes, I assumed they had tiny shoes, brown leather I thought, and matching jackets, no, waistcoats, like in the old days when men used to wear hats, they looked so smart, my uncle wore a hat like that, but he didn't look smart, he looked in charge though, but he worked alone, not like these little men, they work together to box up all of your memories and then when you need to know something, one of them runs and finds the right box and puts it in the knowing machine, and then you know it again and then he puts it back, in alphabetical order of course, they are all very tidy people, they have to be, anyway there's a section in the back of your brain that all the secret memories are stored, there's a guard and he looks after them, because we don't want to know them, that's why they are in the secret section, and this man, he doesn't sleep, he just guards, very still, I imagine he has a moustache, a huge one that curls at the end, but one day he goes on a bathroom break, very quick, and one of the other workers throws what I imagine is a baseball, they have to have some fun too you know, but this ball, it hits one of my secret boxes and breaks it into a thousand pieces and I'm just standing there, talking because I've always liked to talk, and suddenly I stopped, I just stopped.

Two Round Arcs Bisected by a Central Line

David Greaves

OF COURSE THERE are benefits despite it being the wrong habitat for my work. Looking out in the warm evenings over the rippling mud water and feeling the air vibrate (plucked strings almost) with the insect calls is irreplaceable. Some find the heat and in particular the humidity uncomfortable but I have never felt that way. And the moon above the foliage – cloned, dissected in the water's surface: that is beautiful to see.

We moved in around six months ago but it was some time before I became aware of the tensions. The drive took two days and although the heat pressed us near to choking nobody snapped. We talked almost constantly, mostly Jamie, my stitches were uncomfortable although it's better since they were removed. Jamie talked and I tried to concentrate on what he was saying but it was difficult. When we arrived the first thing I did was drink a glass of water and collapse into a chair.

During the week I see very little of Claire and Jamie. Their schedules have an isolating effect and I have my own routine to follow. Initially, though, everything seemed calm. And I had never seen any strains before, they seemed perfectly aligned which was one of the reasons I agreed to join them here; I could not have dealt with significant fractures. Then the house itself was an incentive. It's attractively spacious and there is a sense of age to it, a certain solidity. I wondered if it dated from the colonial era but apparently it does not. After we moved in Claire and Jamie went for a number of drives to get to know the area but I preferred to stay with the house.

It is pleasantly furnished; the soft carpets in particular are a relief at the end of the day. When I get home I like to sit for a little while with my feet in warm water then walk downstairs, sit on the couch with my bare feet on the carpet and push my toes into its deep pile. There is a television in the living room but I don't watch it unless there happens to be a programme which relates to my work. Often I'm sitting here when Claire gets back and wakes Jamie. Sometimes she says hello but a lot of the time she's too tired. Recently I've heard their voices more often, I suppose they must be arguing.

A collective of honeybees with a single hive is a colony. The cascade of their bodies viscous and so golden. Lately the bees have shown more of an interest in me personally. I watch them form a cloud around my hands often. I have remarked on it to my colleagues who have taken notes on this unusual behaviour. The way they diffuse out of the hive which sits organic and pulsing and sweet. In every other respect, however, they continue to behave normally. I see them furious among the flowers and so watch their waggle dance.

When I heard them arguing for the first time I decided to spend the evening outside. The lazy air tangling with evening sun and swamp birds on the wing was almost enough to drown out the sound of their shouting which I have never been able to bear. Claire had just got back and hadn't spoken to me. I was absorbed in a journal anyway although I don't remember which (this happens sometimes). Claire walked upstairs and I heard voices but couldn't make out the words. I continued to read for a moment then walked outside. In the quiet I could hear insects clicking across the swamp. There were a few moths swarming around the outside light which after a second I switched off. I stared out I suppose not looking at anything in particular while sullen fish circled the swamp for specks of prey. Roots gnarled and crept into the water. There are few flowers there and I found the limited play of colours seductive.

Very occasionally I will drink a glass of wine with or (as is more often the case) after a meal. This is the extent of my alcohol consumption but in the past I have indulged both more frequently and widely, I have several bottles of mead in a case left over from a previous Christmas. If I drink, I try and make the glass last as long as I can, then when I've finished I leave it on a flat surface until I think I'm able to wash it without breaking anything. I don't believe Claire or Jamie share this habit but I don't often see them drink so I can't be sure. Although I dislike beer there have been times when I've been intrigued enough to sample it. Once when I was on holiday in England I encountered a beer made with honey. It was named for the waggle dance which honeybees perform to communicate the location of new sources of pollen. Karl von Frisch was one of the first to translate the meaning of the dance. I wrote a thesis on his work. It is beautiful to think that through my vocation I have a link to such a man.

Once, Jamie came into my room when he got home from work. It was earlier than I normally get up but that day I was staying at home to work on a report and so I didn't mind. I think he was drunk. His words were slurred and his hands were shaking a little. His knuckles were torn to pieces. He didn't say much that I understood because I'd just woken up but I remember him talking about the swamp. He was talking about plants that grow at the bottom living on just the smallest amount of sunlight never knowing maybe even that they're underwater. I was surprised because before he had never shown the slightest interest in botany. He didn't look at me while he talked and eventually he stood up and went to bed. Then for a couple of hours I went back to sleep.

I have heard a hypothesis that honeybees can perceive interactions on a quantum level and in this way perceive changes in electromagnetic fields and communicate these in the dance. This hypothesis is laughable of course but seductive. The beauty of the bees' movements and it would yes it would be beautiful to think that they are rooted so fundamentally in the wider universe if that even makes sense. What if there is no wider existence than the life of a honeybee? All things are described in its movements in its perfect life I see nectar in all things yes clamouring to be drunk.

I have placed flowers next to all the windows at the front of the house and left these windows open but so far they have attracted no attention. I need to remember to shut the windows before I go to sleep because as Claire rightly points out it is dangerous not to. I think there may be larger animals in the swamp although I'm not sure what.

I focus best when I work in the small study upstairs at the front of the house. The window is narrow but adequate for me to see outside, not that I spend much time looking when I'm working. I keep flowers there too and their scent, I think, aids me in my work. It conjures the sense of immediacy and visceral reality I feel when in the field.

I do listen to music when I work, most often to Bach, I have not yet made my way past the Goldberg Variations. My favourite recordings are Glenn Gould's (1955) and Maria Yudina's (1968). For obvious reasons many people ask how I feel about Rimsky-Korsakov but I don't feel I understand his intentions particularly since it is clear to anyone who gives it a second of thought that not only would a honeybee have been a far more suitable and poetic subject but also that the flight of any bee is in terms of complexity and beauty far beyond the ability of any individual to capture, at least honestly, at least respectfully. Its wings blur either side of the bars. Its eyes confuse the ear, synesthetic, they reflect every key. Thirty-four million years of existence in its present form alone cannot be expressed in the terms of these human conventions and I do not intend this as a slight of Rimsky-Korsakov, it is simply that the subject is too wide for his grasp.

So the piece aggravates me and if I were to listen to it while trying to work it would likely distract me, the frantic violins would no doubt cascade and lodge in the floorboards and the scratches in the desk, I would feel cramped, really the study is too small for a piece like that.

I have begun rereading Karl von Frisch's papers at night as a means of aiding sleep. I find his doctoral thesis on minnows interesting but only as a sideline. It doesn't spark my imagination in the same way his later masterpieces do. It intrigues me, though, that his initial work concerned such a different topic, it seems almost incomprehensible but of course it is good to remember that in life we may find ourselves on unexpected paths. I sometimes imagine myself talking with Karl von Frisch in the atrium of the University of Munich, leaning over the first-floor railing and watching the paths of the students crisscrossing below us, or perhaps sitting at a table on the street outside a bar with a glass of beer and discussing our work. These things I think of in idle moments.

A honeybee's sense of smell has a spatial element and is slightly but only slightly more attuned to sweet scents than that of a human they know the position of the sun they fly by the earth's magnetic fields aligned like needles true north and their eyes have perhaps a lower resolution than a human's but the facets track movement with more acuity. They cannot tell red from black but they see in ultraviolet therefore patterns in the sky and patterns in the petals of flowers that we may never see with these eyes, or with his, the spectacled eyes that saw this too.

I have yet to meet any of our neighbours or in fact even to see them. The dense foliage around the swamp blocks all surrounding structures from view. At one point I mentioned to Claire that we might go and speak to them but she was busy and tired and didn't respond. I did worry about the physical and mental toll which her and Jamie's work may have on them but have since become reassured they can handle it. They make sure, for example, to eat healthily; there is always fruit in the house and they eschew pre-prepared packaged meals. Sometimes at weekends we drive into the city and have a meal together which is always pleasant, although at times one or the other is too tired to speak or finish their meal. I generally drive the three of us back as on these occasions I do not drink. I have not tried raising the subject of our neighbours on these drives and I have not mentioned at all that I think I have seen one of them at the back of the house at night, the moon shattering off his glasses, echoing in his white hair.

They have been arguing more recently. It is difficult to get to sleep sometimes because Karl von Frisch's work is so engaging, not merely in terms of scientific interest, the literary merit is also undeniable. War hovers over every syllable threatening to burst through and consume his intellect, his passion, but he resists. Sometimes I wonder if the drive behind his work came in some way from his love for his brothers, he was the youngest of four and I can imagine that he wanted his brothers to live in the best world he could give them.

It saddens me sometimes that he didn't live to see the end of the Cold War – a moment he would surely have cherished – but then I think that perhaps he'd seen it already. By the time of his death he had become so adept at reading the waggle dance that he could isolate and read in it the curls of human history. Last week I tried to draw Claire's attention to one of his more beautiful sentences but she seemed distracted, she looked through me for a moment then looked back at her meal and said you know nobody's healed if they're still numb. I nodded, I think I agree.

Unique among bees, with the honeybee a new hive is created not by a single queen but by the new virgin ferocious on royal jelly and a swarm of worker bees from her birth hive. Karl von Frisch found that a new honeycomb's horizontal alignment will be identical to that of the honeycomb in the swarm's home hive. Insignia. And this alignment is so perfect because the earth's magnetic fields guide the bees as they build and as they fly, because they do not know what it means to be lost.

As they cloud around me every time I feel such love such security and want to share their orchestra of perception to fit so well into the earth and, and I think of colony collapse and how I would die yes would die to keep them from that fate to save their perfect order from that chaos. Today under the veil I opened my mouth.

Several times now I have found blood in the sink and, once, a tooth. Jamie's. I haven't asked him about it as I'm sure he will talk when he's ready, and then probably to Claire, they are closer to each other than I will ever be and that is the way it should be although it is undeniably useful at times to have someone else to talk to. The nights are drawing in colder now. I take honey in my tea, of course, and watch from the back of the house nearly every night. The moon is intoxicating. I think our neighbour may be a kindred spirit as he keeps returning and given the dark and the distance it's impossible to tell whether or not we've made eye contact yet but I'm almost certain we have; given our respective alignments both to one another and the water it seems inevitable. I've made some guesses as to his identity based on certain physical mannerisms and general appearance but it's too early to tell.

This weekend we went to a restaurant again and Jamie collapsed at the end of the starter, I'm not sure whether through the wine or lack of sleep. I suppose most likely a mix of both. It was quite dark, candlelit with some unobtrusive lamps set into indents in the walls. The *maître d'* was extremely professional and the waiter was friendly. Claire made an effort to respond to his jokes in kind but Jamie's eyes were unfocused and she was distracted. I drank tap water and looked around at the other tables briefly then waited for my meal to arrive. Jamie was having trouble remaining upright and his facial expression was unusual. Whenever his eyes were open he kept them fixed on me as if he couldn't be sure I was there.

I was upset as I had enjoyed the starter very much, crawfish, and was looking forward to the chicken but Claire felt strongly that we should leave, she paid and I left a generous tip. On the drive back she spoke a lot but I didn't really catch any of it and I think it was probably mostly meant for Jamie's ears anyway. When we got back she took him to bed and I watched videos of hive construction set to Bach.

The bees get so close I could count each speck of pollen on their legs soon they will be sluggish I know we will find the bodies of the drones littered outside the hive. But it is not winter yet and they are still eager, if I could get as close as Karl von Frisch then he would be impressed oh envy is an ache and when I get home the smell on my skin is that of honey.

Jamie came home late. Claire was waiting for him and I heard them arguing, I wondered why they couldn't wait just a few hours, eventually I got up and went to watch the dawn at the back, sky slowly morphing into day. He was there and left before the light grew strong enough for me to see him but I'm sure anyway, I know who he is. Jamie had left his shoes by the front door and when I walked upstairs I nearly stood on them which would have been dangerous because there was broken glass embedded in the soles, I should mention that to him. I didn't go back to sleep and eventually went to my study to work, occasionally glancing at the sun through the petals, imagining the dash of ultraviolet.

Jamie didn't go to work today. He and Claire began arguing almost the moment she got home, the sound of their screaming is like a buzzing inside my head, I stayed in my study through most of it but eventually became hungry, went downstairs and after eating stayed at the back of the house. I think he's out there. I can't work in this noise, after all. Soon whatever trigger they are hiding behind will collapse and they will sink and sit, quiet. I tried honeycomb in my tea today. One of my colleagues swears by it but I don't feel more relaxed. Jamie has taken to calling this house our little colony. It bothers Claire and strikes me as fanciful.

The moon is out now and sleeting again onto his glasses. He'll be interested, I think, to hear about my work. I'll have to walk through the swamp to get to him but there are shallow areas and I'm no stranger to heavy boots after all, although in these bulky clothes the lingering humidity is fierce. His stillness is an encouragement. My heart is fluttering and I can smell honey. The buzzing is getting stronger and moving through my skull. I can just about see his face which I think is smiling, I was right. That tingling in my fingers like hundreds of little legs. Their beautiful bodies squirming now formed from the flesh of my throat. Yes and my legs could be stems twirling into a beautiful flowering. Now it is hard to move but I think he will come to me, I think he will. New drones clasped together in place of my tongue. Blink a thousand lidless compound eyes. The nebulae of ultraviolet. Bones of my arms combing themselves into an insignia so royal. I knew he was smiling knew I was right. Yes I want to tell him yes still staring yes as I feel my heart uncoil into a waking queen.

DARKNESS AND THE DARK

Matt Owen

AT THE TOP of the path I'm greeted by two women whose names would surely sound beautiful if I could pronounce them. Smiling sweetly they hand me champagne. *Spasibo,* I say, offering my broken Russian like a cheap fig leaf. *Spasibo.*

Beyond them, away from the gravel trail and through the drooping branches of the birch trees, a crowd swells across the lawn. It's all suits and dresses and writhes silkily. At the top of the hill sits the house, a brilliant white even after nightfall. On the top floor of the house, the curtains are drawn. On the porch there are wooden seats. The seats are empty.

Seventy-two hours ago, a woman bent over an acoustic guitar and sang us gypsy songs. The songs were centuries old and some of the women cried. Through her tears, one of them told me that just as she doesn't believe in God but continues to pray, she doesn't believe in ghosts but thinks that Leo Tolstoy still walks the grounds of Yasnaya Polyana. Standing now, sipping champagne beneath the house's shadowed silhouette, I realise that her tears were right; that if there were ever walls that held ghosts, it is these ones.

The lawn finds me and I am quickly amongst the perfume and cuff-links. It is a social orgy of privileged Europeans with well-carved accents. The buffet is a mile long. People smoke as though it won't kill them, their exhalations unwinding into a coal-black sky studded with stars. They drink. I drink. Despite the bodies, there is little warmth. Somewhere out in the woods where the stray dogs sleep Tolstoy lies in an unmarked grave.

To one side, a careful distance from the knots of chattering well-to-dos, the finishing touches are being applied to a stage. There is to be a performance, an adaptation by a German theatre group of Tolstoy's little-known play, *The Light that Shines in the Darkness*. Twenty-four hours earlier, the director, Hermann, told me through the glow of his iPhone that he is in love with the play because he 'gets it'. Looking at the stage now, I see stone-faced men with barrel-arms carrying crates from right to left, swearing.

I'm being introduced to people, all of whom think I'm here because I have a job to do and not because I have a skill for riding coattails. By my shoulder is my mother, who is the reason I'm wandering forlorn after ghosts in this too-big country. Twenty-four years earlier, I was born into a charmed life to parents who showed me the world through the prism of books. Now, in my poshest voice, I explain numbly that yes I'm a big fan of Tolstoy's work and yes I'm looking forward to the play. 'He wrote it in there, you know; he wrote everything in there,' a man pouts, gesturing towards the house, with its empty chairs. A tepid joke I don't really mean to make is met with a chorus of raucous laughter. I hate my plastic mannerisms, they wear me down, but I go on smiling emptily like everyone else because there is nothing else. A minister of some sort, a woman with bronzed cheeks and pearl earrings, smiles at me with what can only be described as bedroom-eyes and intones 'You absolutely must try the veal, it's wonderful,' and I smile back joylessly and tell myself we love different things.

I'm wandering again, drawn towards the little lamps that necklace through the trees beyond the lawn. At the buffet I leave the veal wallowing in its fleshy sweat, but a young man with marble-like cheekbones offers me more champagne and I accept with another *spasibo* before tipping the stuff into my lungs. Only then do I notice them, the colony of tray-bearers, wandering between elbows and proffering wine. Their eyes flicker with terror at balancing trays. As I sidle behind one of the marquees, I'm met by a pair of them, a boy and a girl, crouched on their haunches passing a bottle between them. They see me and freeze, and I grin, thinking that beneath our clothes we're made of the same stuff, that we can share little crimes because we understand one another, because we believe the same things. But my smile isn't returned. There's just blankness, and them bundling their bottle under an apron and retreating from my gaze.

I'm nearly at the tree-line, where the lamps hang meekly in the gloom, when word drifts across the lawn that the play is to start. My gaze is fixed on the brow of the hill, on the house inhabited by the ghost that even the woman who doesn't believe in ghosts believes in. It's a majestic white, luminescent under the moon. Its windows are shuttered. Vines creep up its walls like ancient fingers. I want to go on staring. In fact really I want to climb up onto the roof and stare out across the whole estate, across the fields which over a century later are still chewed up by peasants and emaciated donkeys, across the fly-bitten lakes where the stray dogs bathe, and across the village in the distance where the roofs peel with paint and where champagne has never flowed. I want to stare like this for hours, and remember the dead. But there is the play, the play Hermann 'gets', and in any case I am too drunk to climb in this darkness.

Off-balance, I head towards the stage. On the way I swipe another drink from another floating tray. I shuffle along the row and wrap myself in the woolly blanket which is folded neatly atop my seat. I balance my wine between my knees. My mother is nowhere to be seen. Behind me, I hear someone whisper, not for the first time, 'a million Euros, the EU grant for this.' In the next instant, the heavy curtains are whisked apart and a boom of footsteps sounds at the left of the stage. The crowd is plunged into darkness. There are English language programmes underneath the seats, and I read mine by the humming light of my iPhone in tandem with the barked German of the actors.

Nicholas: I used to live thus – that is to say, without thinking why I lived; but the time came when I was aghast. We live on the labour of others, we make others work for us… What did I live for? To be a parasite like this?

I realise, from his words, and from the fact that the German playing him is sporting a long, ashen beard, that Nicholas is in fact Tolstoy, just as Levin is Tolstoy in that greatest of great novels. In the front row, under the stage lights, fake-tanned faces are slack with boredom. I go on squinting at the square of light cast by my iPhone, which was put together by bleeding fingers on the other side of the planet.

Nicholas: Here you are, healthy young men and women. You slept till ten
o'clock. Then you had food and drink, and you are still eating, and you
play and discuss music. And there, where I have just come from, the
people are up at three in the morning. Some have not slept at all, having
watched the cattle all night, and all of them, even the old, the sick, and the
children, work with their utmost strength, that we may enjoy the fruits of
their labour.

At the bottom of the estate, in the village of Yasnaya Polyana, the burnt-out
husks of cars litter the roadside and families collect rainwater. They stare at
the well-fed foreigners from behind tired eyes, and at night they can see the
lights dancing at the top of the hill.

Nicholas: We have all robbed the people, have stolen their land, and then we
instituted a law against stealing. And the church sanctions it all.

In Moscow, the hungry sleep on benches and Lenin lies under Red Square,
pumped full of wax, just another failed prophet.

Nicholas: I cannot go on living like this; I cannot endure this horrible life of
depravity. The money we live on comes from the land we have stolen from
the people. Today I saw a child dying of starvation; and I come home and a
footman in a white tie opens my front door to me.

Outside Moscow, on the sides of the road, men with trucks full of
watermelons stare at passing limousines.

Nicholas: I cannot come home and see a Christmas tree, a ball, hundreds
squandered, when others are dying of hunger. I cannot live like this.

Have mercy on me. I am worn out. Let me go. Good-bye.

The play ends with a sudden swell of artificial light. There is a pause, some
whispered hesitation, and then a pattering of applause. Some of Tolstoy's
latter-day descendants file before the front of the stage, grinning with delight
and waving at the crowd, which claps harder at the sight of something it can
understand. Hermann is there, 'getting it', resplendent in a double-breasted
suit. The actors bow modestly and begin to file away, peeling off their disguises.

I spill wine over my shoes. *A million Euros.* Everyone shakes off their woolly blankets and stands. The chatter resumes. The stage quickly begins to come down, and the swarm drags me back towards the buffet. Around me, people call their drivers.

I end up in another ring of anonymous dignitaries. The talk is diffuse. The play was excellent, they all agree, quite the performance, and the food too, sublime, not forgetting the veal, the local veal no less, just sublime, and the whole organisation of the thing, just brilliant, especially without the rain, how lucky we are. I nod along, wanting deeply to believe that I am somehow duplicitous when in fact I'm just another suit smoking as though it won't kill me. Somewhere in the woods, where the stray dogs roam, Tolstoy is part of the soil. Above me, the stars burn in the freezing sky. Breathing steam, I spill more wine on my shoes just as I realise there is a Russian Orthodox priest standing next to me, sombre-faced.

'Did you enjoy the play?' he asks, catching my eye.

I'm either well on the way to being truly drunk now, or that's the weight of God's hand I can feel on me.

'Yes,' I nod nervously. 'I enjoyed it very much.'

'Yes. I did also. Lyev was a great man. He did some good things for the people. It is a source of regret for me, a source of deep regret, that he had such troubles. No-one ever really made him happy, I don't think. There's so *much* none of us know about a person, isn't there? Even when we're staring right at them?'

'There certainly is,' I reply.

I need to get away again, away from the exhausting brouhaha and the priest's omen and my treachery, when a girl in a dizzyingly long dress meets my gaze and demands to know who I am. She stands demurely, with her legs crossed at the ankles and her chin floating in harmony with her neck. Her stare is lazy. I tell her my name and then a stream of pointless lies, not because I have any desire to impress her, but because this whole party is a lie, and I'm the biggest lie of all, and if what I'm witnessing is a bonfire of legacies then I might as well add my matchstick. In a painfully Oxbridge voice she informs me with faux modesty that she is the great man's great-great-grand-daughter, or perhaps great-great-grand-niece. I am too full of booze to be surprised. I notice now the tiny gems that riddle her earrings and the single silver ring that balloons across her knuckles. Her friends, mannequins given life just like myself, laugh at something else I say that isn't funny. She tells me that the play is one of her favourites, at which the others nod, and instead of screaming or crying at our absurdity I lie some more in my poshest voice. With my heart heavy as a landmine I listen to her talking about an array of things that don't matter to anyone except her, as is obligatory for girls whose idea of love is missionary sex in a hall of mirrors. She invites me to go riding the next morning. Straight-faced, I accept, knowing I will never see her again. At my acceptance there are more bedroom-eyes, or at least what my sad soul tells me are bedroom-eyes, and for the first time in my life I feel like the stable-boy, except I'm the pathetic stable-boy, the miscast stable-boy who can't ride a horse and who even if he wanted to wouldn't fuck the rich girl because it would taste like dancing on a grave.

'More champagne, we should get more champagne. There's some better stuff inside, come on, all of you, follow me.'

Winter knows no host like Mother Russia. The cold is like needles across the skin as we all trot lazily up the lawn towards the house, shrouded in shadow.

'Stay here, I'll be back.'

My wallet is stuffed with cards too, and half a continent away I sleep comfy too, and this is the worst thing. Against the sky, the front of the house looms up in front of me, blindingly white, and I know that the old woman was right, that God may be dead but ghosts still walk this land even if they're unknown to us.

I cannot live like this. Have mercy on me. I am worn out. Let me go.

She vanishes through the front door, and in that instant I tell myself it isn't so. In silence, with the moon hanging heavy in the sky like a celestial candle, I leave the girls to their chatter and the priest to his regret. At the buffet I fill my pockets. Then I walk blindly in the direction of Tolstoy's grave, and between the trees amongst that darkness I toss veal to the dogs.

THE LAST HOURS OF KNOWING

Amy Nicholls-Diver

Summer had just slipped away
and a sly wind crept through columns of concrete
on the stark construction site
to find me as I searched for you.
My call went to your message-bank.
Once, twice, three times over.

But I tried not to know, and reached out to life
a little more.
And so I brushed my hand
against the hands of another,
whose skin was warm.
I was desperate to know
something other than I knew.

I knew when our dad hadn't heard from you either.
On the train rumbling quietly home,
We told untruths across the telephone lines.
'I'm sure she's fine.'
It seemed silly to cry, with nothing yet
To cry for.

Later, from his home to mine,
my uncle rang.
Did his voice crackle
when he said he'd had better days?

He didn't tell me anything
but I knew a little more.

I ran a hot bath.
I could always breathe a little better, in the warmth –
did we share that, I wonder,
a prenatal bond?
We shared that same first space, years apart.

The knock on the door came.
My dressing-gown clung to damp skin like truth,
as I hurried to answer.

He looked so small,
standing on the doormat, his shoulders curved in,
like mine,
like yours.

'Our baby's gone,'
he said, and stepped inside.
His grief filled my living room
My chest contracted.
I didn't know anything

After all.

LIVING

Samuel Dodson

SHE TOLD ME that she had a dream I was dying. Dying in a pool of blood, she said. In a field of torn bodies, she said. In war, she said. And she said that it felt as if she was giving birth to me. Yet that it was with a pain that crushed her rather than set her free. She told me and I said that it was just a dream; that I wasn't going to die. That there was no war on and in any case if there was I wouldn't join the army because I wasn't patriotic and didn't want to die for anyone who asked me to fight for a country I didn't believe in. But she told me she had seen the wounds in my flesh, had felt it in her throat as I choked on blood. She was blinded as my sight left me and had ached as my lungs tore themselves apart inside me. I said I had to go to work.

I took up the full time post Mister Solomon offered me as a joiner. Each day on my way to work I would walk beside the field where the gypsies camped. The gypsy horses grazed and in summer the wild flowers came alive with insects which hovered sweetly in the air. I would return home in the evening and cut the potatoes and carrots from our garden and my mother would prepare the rest of the food and we would sit together at the wooden table, side by side, and look out of the window past our little garden to the graveyard where my father was buried. I would wait till she had finished her food and then begin to clear the plates and cutlery away, and she would tell me she had dreamt that I had died again. I would tell her that I had not died and she would not say another word as I washed what needed to be cleaned and left to have a drink with Rory at the Arms.

Then one day she wouldn't help me prepare the meal, and wouldn't accept the food I put out in front of her. She said nothing. She looked at her food and at nothing else and I tired of waiting for her to start and ate my own and asked her why she would say nothing and not eat. And she started to cry. She didn't make any noise and the tears she wept clung to her cheek and froze there. And so I stood and went across to her and put my hands on her shoulders and kissed the top of her head and suddenly she gasped outward and moaned terribly and she shuddered in my arms and she begged me to leave her, she said that she couldn't see me because I had died and she asked me not to stay with her because she couldn't see me because I was dead. So I left to join Rory at the pub.

As autumn began to course through the trees, I started walking through the graveyard rather than beside the field which the gypsies had camped in. From the moment they had left the field I felt a coldness on the inside of my stomach if I walked my old route. The grass beside the path appeared grey and the individual blades seemed to lose their clarity and definition. Footsteps became muted by an empty sigh that crept from the field. And if the wind passed over, it carried with it the sound of the gypsy horses.

The graveyard held in its confines the lost limbs and names of ten generations of people from the village. The church had been destroyed a century ago and no new one built, so burial ceremonies were taken by Mister Thompson, as he was the only person in the village to have ever read the Holy Book. Only people born in the village were buried here. There had once been a traveller who came from the East who had taken up residence here in the generation before mine. He had died one night in a storm. The oak which had grown in his garden had blown over onto his house and crushed him in his bed. No one would bury him in the graveyard or touch his corpse, so they heaped tonnes of earth over his house; creating the tumulus which now stands on the outskirts of the village.

I never stray from the central path in the graveyard. I never see my father's grave. His name hangs on my breath yet lacks the substance to form on my lips and tongue as sound. The large crypts and Celtic crosses which line the central avenue emit a warmth which coats and comforts my skin. As I leave the graveyard I carry the warmth home and back to my house where I find my mother standing on the landing looking out through the upstairs window. She stands motionless and says nothing as the wind brushes the long grass in waves which float gently through the fields as if it were a calm sea.

One morning before sunrise my mother begins to scream. Her voice breaks the particles of my bones. She screams day and night for two days. Our corner of the street is avoided and people mutter that my mother is cursed. Their muttering and whispering fills the village and shakes the branches of the trees with its weight. Birds stop flying over the village. The pigeons which belonged to Mister Carr fly away and do not return. Mister Donovan's two sheepdogs are found beside the river in the forest; dead, as if frozen by an inner turmoil. My mother stands in her room screaming at the same pitch and I stand beside her, holding her shoulders and trying to soothe her with my voice, letting the shadow of my breath warm her ear.

After she stops screaming she becomes silent. Her eyes turn inwards. I return to work, yet she takes to dead-bolting the front door so I have to nip in through the back garden and squeeze myself through the kitchen window, prizing it open using a thin stick. Susan Ellis in the house next to ours watches me break into my house from her bedroom window and I smile at her and she blushes and flashes a perfect set of teeth between her subtle lips.

As winter deepens in our veins, our work increases and I leave for home in the dark, walking with a handheld lantern through the streets of the village as I make my way to the graveyard. With tendrils of night skating across my skin, I'm stopped beside the coach house by Miss Karla whose husband had left for America and died on the journey over there. She dressed in clothes from the city and sold her wedding ring when she heard her husband had died. She asks me to help fix her door so that it will close. She shows me to her house and as I stand on a small stool to fix the joinery of her door she puts a hand on my hip. I look into her eyes and I see.

I walk home that night stepping quickly over the cobbles with the stink of it still on me. I jump into the kitchen and into my mother's room and I feel it on my breath. My mother stands and shouts that I am dead again and I say I am not dead mother, I am alive, and she screams and tells me that blood is pouring out of my mouth and my teeth are loosening in my gums as they decay and she can see the death rising beneath my eyeballs and my skin tightening and there is blood on my clothes and my hand is gripping to a hand which has left me.

She paces across to me and spits in my eye, and I strike her across the cheek with my hand. The coarseness of my hand cuts her face and she gasps and falls to the floorboards. She puts a fingertip to her cheek and she tastes the blood and looks at me and I tell her to see; that is what real blood tastes like.

I leave straight for the graveyard and begin to look for my father's grave. The warmth from the graves lingers over me, drapes across my shoulders. I inspect each grave yet cannot find my father's. It's not possible for me to know if this is because he isn't buried here or because I'm unable to remember his name. I prop my lantern against a Celtic cross and sit down beside it, crossing my legs. It begins to snow. Each snowflake settles securely on the limestone. I open my mouth and let snow fill in the space between my tongue and gums. The back of my neck is warm. I look to the sky and the stars aren't there.

So my father wasn't buried in the graveyard. Or his name had finally left my memory completely. The last strands of it severed from my mind, cut out from my vocabulary and thoughts. My mother is found one day walking through the wood, almost naked. Mister Thompson says she has seen the devil. I take a few days off work and spoon-feed her watery soup as she lies in bed. Once, she starts at the touch of the liquid to her lips and looks at me, I smile at her, but she closes her eyes and cries.

Rory begins to go out with Eileen Jones. She sits with us at the pub whilst we talk beside the fire place. She listens to us carefully, not saying anything that would jeopardise her relationship with Rory, for Rory was inclined to go cool on her if he thought she was trying to undermine him in front of me. One evening before spring, she tells us she heard war was coming. Rory says that he will fight, that he isn't afraid to die, that he is ready to kill another human being. I tell him that he is not old enough to fight anyway, that the king is not ours to fight for. Rory says that he'll be of age by the time war comes – if it's coming at all – and that we should fight together as brothers on the battlefield. We shake hands and laugh and he buys us two more drinks.

Three nights before my eighteenth birthday my mother slips into a thirty-six hour sleep. When she wakes she sees me and asks if I can fetch her some food and a drink of water. She smiles as I return with what she asked for and she touches the side of my face. She tells me that she dreamt about the day she gave birth to me. How I had cried so loudly the doctor had left the room, but how I had stopped the moment my mother had stroked my cheek with the back of her finger.

My mother tells me that she loves me and I return the phrase. I look out of the window and watch a bird fly down and land in the bird bath in our garden.

The summer heat brings the insects back to the field flowers. The grass grows strong and defined, but the gypsies never return. On the evening of my birthday I walk with Susan Ellis into the field and we lie down, hidden by the grass. She feels small in my arms and her breath is soft. It is the longest day of the year; the sun doesn't seem to set at all. In the morning we wake and stay together in the grass, she asks if I will go to war with Rory. I say that I will stay with her and she grips my hand.

The next weekend my papers arrive. I burn them in the fire. Mister Thompson calls round and asks to see my mother. He stays in her room with the door locked for several hours. When he leaves he bumps into me on the landing and pushes something into his pocket hurriedly. He says that the devil is still with my mother. I go into the room after he has left the house and she is crying dry tears. She says she can see the blood on my clothes, and that she saw me in the field. She says that she cannot feel me anymore. She says that she has given birth to a ghost.

A man comes and tells me that if I don't report to the barracks with him now he will arrest me and I will be shot. He has a pale pink royal insignia on his uniform as if blood had brushed fresh snow. I ask if I can say goodbye to Susan and he says yes, I can. I knock on her door but she doesn't answer and the man tells me that he doesn't have the time, that I have to come with him now. As I walk with him away from my street, we pass Mister Thompson and the man nods to him. At the barracks I see Rory getting into the back of a troop transport lorry. He smiles and waves at me. I salute him as he disappears through the gate of the barracks.

On the third day of basic the man who sleeps in the bed next to mine loses his fingers when his rifle misfires. I look at him and see him counting time in his head silently as he stares at the blood covering his mutilated hand. As he reaches thirty seconds he opens his mouth and the terror grips him and he falls on his back and flails and writhes on the floor and has to be restrained by two others. But they hold his chest too tight and they don't realise he's having an asthma attack and he dies there, in the training field. And I lay awake that night looking at the shrouded ceiling and see nothing and everything as the memory of what the stars look like tethers itself around a part of my brain I had forgotten existed and I remember the look on my father's face as he sat me on top of the gypsy horse and dappled sunlight fell on my eyes.

As I take my first post as night watchman I read the letter I had been given in the morning. It is from Rory, he tells me that he is well and has been promoted to sergeant. He says he wishes we were fighting side by side and that when we get some leave he will buy me a pint. He asks if I have heard any news from the village. I fold the letter and put it into my chest pocket next to my cigarettes. My breath rises in front of my eyes and as I rub my hands together someone arrives and tells me my shift is over.

I engrave a phrase into my rifle, 'We destroyed ourselves with machines. Tore our bodies apart with cruel manufactured metals. The fields are ravaged and beaten, and forests are uprooted.' They say that we are fighting against evil. They shot MacInnes when he said this war was pointless, that we were victims of imperialism. A young boy's dead form has twisted around itself and he looks up at me from a hole in the ground. His face is a distant memory. The field is full of nameless dead who will not be buried. I look out across hell as the sun begins to rise and I think of my father.

LILLY, POLLY & THE BLIND FISHERMAN

Conrad Bird

Can you pull in the Leviathan with a fishhook
or tie down his tongue with a rope? (Job 41:1)

i pub

The fish market was foul with rot; festering mackerel
had lost their rainbow sheen & were rankled with lice.

The sea-bass, normally full & broad with sprat, squelched
under fishmongers' knives; a mush of over-ripe blood & meat.

The breakers lifted their hunched backs, gorged with thick tide-
    broth,
& the stone-rakkle rapped down the sand gullets:

Frenzied Atlantic swells, chopping like swine at swill,
had not let the whalers from the harbour wall for weeks.

Angus the creel man, loaded with mac & dram,
announced to the depressed anglers of Pollachar Inn:

'Och tmmorro ai go, yu wotch, mi nets ll full tu the brum wi bug
    beestis.
yon moanin' seas a butch orra bairn an needs a whllopin'!'

The Blind Fisherman grinned machete into his MacAndrew beer,
& quietly said through a plume of blue pipe smoke

'The sea is a swarm of swooping gulls, hungry for fresh placenta.
Do not take your boat out before Thursday, a bit of friendly advice.'

His eyes are blind with brine & salt, bare & hollow.
For ten years the wound has been rebuilding the world

inside his head: the mountains, Hecla and Beinn Mhor,
stand statue in his brain; the peat-bog brooks gurgle down the
    gorge

of his throat; the heather mossed moors fur his lungs
& the sea raves from the depth of his intestine. His lust is the sun on
    his skin,

the moon is the eclipse he is caught in; a net that cuts up his vision
into a thousand triangles of twisted twine. 'Thursday,' he murmurs.

   ii thursday morning

He sets the gas mark to high-tide & lets the coffee roll.
The grit settles on the kettle's bed like pebbles in surf boil.

He hears the sea over the trees, the pull & exhale
of Lilly's heavy morning breath. It yawns through

his bone-curled conch & his ear opens with the sea-bored holes
of Staffa. Waves rush through his branches,

flooding the nooks and knuckles of cartilage: an insistent osss –
the grey bone crunch he knows will fill his day.

Troops of tractors, gull-bannered, salt-corroded
*boeotia*n mammoths plough the still-blue fields of peat.

Their tyres spin with dew like Boudicca's scythed chariots.
Five o'clock: the sun has not warmed the sky –

the cloud's bloated fish bellies are still full with bones
shells   cuttlefish   clams   & the half-digested sprat of night-light.

Thursday morning lies flat, warm
& incarcerated. The Atlantic fronts crumble

like fresh bread on a porcelain dish. The Blind Fisherman
looks over his shoulder feeling the mist un-plait across the east;

it spangles with sky reflection on the furrowed sea,
& ripples against the roof of his skull.

Polly whirs through the straits of South Uist to Lingay:
yachts carve on skims of surf –
                                                peregrines tack the sky.

The topaz flits like a kingfisher & rowing boats skull the water
with the heavy wiping metronome of heron wing.

But Polly wobbles, a fat seagull perturbed by a salt ridden wind,
hacking & heaving on oil against the haul of the sea.

    iii fishing

He trawls the coral troughs, spinning between the gnarled rock
    fingers
for mackerel & pollack. Sea-swallows oar-stroke above the surf-

slammed gullies, their delicate fanned wings reflecting the
  feathered lures,
bobbing like buoys in storm or the boulder heads of scouting
  seals.

The fish line sings like a mosquito, slicing fresh wounds
into his scarred palms; a mountain range of river-runs

& bloody valleys. The sea-blast stings his hook cuts
& the spray slimes his skin with brine-sweat.

He whistles a hauling song as he casts; Donal Agus Morag –
but the strips of tune are gut-sucked by the wind-demons

like crab claw down throat. All our Blind Fisherman has to guide
  him,
through the channels and slopes of water, is the high bleep of his
  fish-finder

& the eyes and bark of his bitch, Lilly of the West.
All he can do is stare millions of miles past the horizons

that smart in the sun, & carve a sight from his silent vision
with a deeper consciousness
            than thought.

  iv breath

The day's catch of fish & crab thrash in the keel
banging their briny blood over the boat, sloppy

with the gunge of scales & gut. 'Enough,'
the Blind Fishermen thinks out loud to Lilly

who is slyly pulling at the flesh of a fat pollack.
'We have bait. Now we can move further out, where the monsters be.'

As Polly splutters through the opening ocean,
the crests rising like clusters of cone trees
in thickening forests, darkness pulls across the water.
The front holds off, like horses recovering from a race

& the Northern Lights dance in Lilly's glassy eyes; a rare glimpse
into the glittering landscape of her master's inner globe.

No lamps are lit; he only needs the feel of the line –
the hand over hand, the wave over a wave

like shifting horizons dividing grey from grey.
The tug of the tide tightens & slacks the rope in easy rhythm,

the sea slaps & licks against Polly's body, a still night
of slow love. A loud splash to the left means

that somewhere close
a minke whale is breathing.

   v friday morning

There. Axes at pine; falling, falling again, white fish
like chips & splinter arch away; terns & gulls dig at the sea

for a shoal of pilchards that whisk the waves like boiling milk
planing their flanks in egg and milt.

The morning has opened with frenzy.
The Blind Fisherman revs the outboard into a clanking hum

& follows the glint of the guttural gull squawk,
like shuddering bass thunder among the silver flecks

of a herring school. A hundred feet below something is hunting,
guided by the spiralling judders of fish-fright,

steadily climbing towards the glass glint
of the early sun cutting the sea into mosaic.

Its underbelly is as hard as whetstone, grainy
as the whorl of the pebble-pattern.

Scales lay on scale, rusty with lack of light
& hung with blackened kelp and rockweed.

Its thick tail-fin rudders deliberately
like an oak's heavy mane in a hurricane.

The Blind Fisherman casts his rig; lost for a moment
in a tower of clouds that pillow the sea-hazed sun,

before dropping; swallowed by the thickening swell.
It is his deep religion! Lines to a deeper world

where the blue sky only grows greener as it grows
deeper. Never has the sun seen such deepness.

vi the catch

His body is bent over the side, thick veined,
eyes all sea-stained, measuring up to an unfamiliar weight.

More hands are needed. He has none. Hand over hand.
The rub of running ropes pulls at his reflection

in the water; the taut line connecting him
with a forgotten image of himself.

Lilly's hackles excite as gradually the shadow shapes
beneath the surface. Not struggling in the water

but quite at home there, gazing up through the salt refracted
contortions at a world of colour and clear lines.

Only when the watery thing is warped in, gaffed
& its magenta blood diffuses like a scattering storm

through the thrashed up surf-boil,
does the scramble & struggle & fight begin.

Losing oxygen, its muscle grip on the gaff weakens.
As water torrents from the serrated gills the thing drowns in air

& gives itself up.

vii storm

The Blind Fisherman cocks his head. He catches the smell
of peat that blows like pollen from Ludag & sets his bearing.

Polly, laden with this monster, sits low in the sea & slowly turns
    for land
carving the troughs & crests like blunt knives cut overcooked
    meat.

But he senses a stirring. The air suffers a change of taste.
He can hear the horses.

They whinny in the wind; stamping and snorting.
Their breathless energy, tense and overwrought

with the strain of the calm. They are ready to un-stock.
Here it comes, hackled with electricity.

Mountains rip & curl from the tectonic plates of water,
spray whips & wrangles, strangling anything that is not sea.

Wave after wave after wave, like twists in a rope,
snarl the boat in a net of ravines and peaks –

Polly is plunged deep into the chopping surf, hardly afloat
& it is lost. The blood-slimed body slips unnoticed

into the bowels of the moving ocean;
boiling as lightning splits peels of sky.

The gale passes by evening & curtains of thin rain
flutter across the sea stage, swollen with the remnants of tempest.

Words slump like a sinking coastland,
headlands slide into the white silence of the sea.

THE BIRDS

Sophie Mackintosh

THE BIRDS ARE evacuating the city. The dock seagulls are tumbling disorientated into the inner suburbs, before flying over the centre and away. The sparrows left in one panicked, pluming flock; from the ground they looked like bees swarming. The pigeons too have already gone and it's surprising how much they are missed. In their absence the rats overspill from the drains as easily as groundwater, unable to believe their luck.

None of us knows why the birds are going and nobody can pinpoint the moment it began. At first they left slowly, a dozen here and there, and during that time only the ornithologists noticed. They came out in the early morning, binoculars strung around their necks, to solemnly watch the sky, skulking damp around the peripheries of parks and scrubland. Articles came out in magazines; newspapers talked vaguely about 'new migration patterns' in the area, or 'mass mating rituals', but you could tell they were grasping at straws. Meanwhile the birds left in greater and greater numbers, so that even the most preoccupied of us took note.

Then came that period of two weeks when the sky was strangled under their weight. We woke up to it, pulling back our curtains to be greeted with the sight of birds upon birds. Birds collaged together and pressed into one giant, ragged-edged bird that wasn't a bird but a cloud blotting out the whole sun. A cloud that writhed and screamed a million birdsongs compressed into one buckling note. Outside, you had to keep your hands pressed against your ears, or wear earplugs; although, admittedly, many people were too afraid to leave the house at all.

People started wearing scuba masks and goggles to the grocery store and carried baseball bats in case of bird attacks. There was something unnerving about bumping into people dressed this way; it was hard to see their eyes behind the fogged-up polycarbonate. The main streets looked like the tail end of a psychotic carnival, everyone dressed in bizarrely assembled armour and swinging umbrellas above their heads. It already seems ridiculous, because the birds weren't interested in anything happening on the ground. They just jostled for sky space, waited for the backlog to clear.

We sheltered from bird feathers for the whole two weeks, as if it were squalling rain that refused to stop. The machines used to clear the parks of leaves were mobilised, the roads closed off as workers gleaned amongst the debris. (Cars themselves were almost unrecognisable; carwashes were experiencing their most profitable fortnight in living memory. Feathers weren't the only thing we were dodging.) There was a lot of public debate about what to do with the feathers. I believe the softer ones were sold cheaply to make pillows and coverlets, while the rest were gathered up and incinerated. You can still catch vague offshoots of tarry smoke all through the night, as they pile up the leftover waste like bonfires, set it ablaze. Damp feathers do not burn well. Meanwhile, in the daytime, children kicked and swam their way through soft furrows of plumage and down. I didn't blame them – if I was their age I would have done the same. Instead I satisfied myself by picking stray feathers from my window box every morning, rubbing them between my fingers. Some left a marbled film on my skin and others smelled sharply of ozone. I wrapped them in paper and put them away, in case they came in useful. Maybe for gifts, or decorations. Or evidence.

The mayor declared it a state of emergency for no reason other than that he was as confused as we were. He made a speech on the evening bulletin about the importance of community and told us to be good to each other, while his face sweated like cheese above his collar. There have been no riots and no major panics. Secretly we are disappointed in the lack of drama. Where are the pre-apocalyptic parties, the smashed windows, the doomsday billboards? There hasn't even been looting. We all agree that we are slightly ashamed by how meekly our city is accepting this potentially cataclysmic event. *If this does portend the end of the world*, we say, *it's really not how I imagined it.*

Each morning at work we gather around the television to catch any news updates. They tailed off for a while after the initial panic, but now the reports from other cities are starting to trickle in (Paris was the latest, this morning; the skies above Edinburgh, Manchester and Leeds are in similar disarray), and nobody even pretends to file or type any more. We make endless cups of tea and flick from channel to channel, scrounging for information. But there is none. All we find is rumour, shards of whisper and conspiracy passed around dark corners and across cyberspace, pieces of adulterated hearsay that tell us nothing.

Now most of the birds seem to have gone, or they are flying with less urgency. They're still trickling out; the lame birds, the slow and old, patiently hefting themselves through the sky. Nests of abandoned eggs rot under the eaves in the heat, and the babies too young to fly were left behind, crying weakly for their parents. The lucky ones are rescued by well-wishers, fed water through eyedroppers, and fly away just like the others as soon as they are able; whatever homing instinct it is that guides them overrides any confusion or fear.

We gather in coffee houses all over the city and wonder what it means. We ask: *what do the birds know that we don't?* After the two weeks of threshing wings, as intrusive as a low-sitting helicopter, silence has the sharpness of glass. We speak softly so as not to disturb the quiet, cupping our ears, repeating ourselves. *Nature is intuitive.* We speak of natural disasters of which erratic animal behaviour was the first warning, sign of vibrations under the ground, staleness in the air. What kind of disaster are the birds portending here? We don't get earthquakes or hurricanes. The sea is at the other end of the city and never rises in a wall of water but just lies there, an insipid streak across the horizon.

Our fear has shifted to an eerie acceptance now that the last of the birds are making their way out of the city. Maybe we are putting on brave faces, or maybe the whole situation just seems too much like a dream. Maybe the birds are so much a part of this city that the idea that they are leaving us is literally unthinkable. Maybe fear will come later on, if it becomes clear they are never coming back. Mostly we are sad. It's an inadequate word but there's no other way to describe it. We gently mourn the loss of our favourite birds. Christmas is coming; what will we do without the robin? Will cards showing a flash of gaudy feather against snow have some kind of undreamed-of poignancy? I'm going to miss the seagulls, the way they fight to the death over salted scraps of newspaper, their unapologetic brashness. Sparrows are too coy and starlings too co-dependent. Others ponder hard over the ones they will miss the most. *Swallows,* one person decides. *I don't even mind them building their nests in my eaves. I feel bad for all the times I minded.* And *kestrels,* another offers, *because seeing one made me feel like I was somewhere else.* We compare collected feathers, splaying them out over Formica tables, around our cups and newspapers, searching for discrepancies. Some have painstakingly recorded every bird sighting, and we compare these too. *One starling: limp, losing feathers. Two jackdaws: glossy, moving quickly. One seagull: young, agitated.*

But for now, the whole city is holding its breath. People are oversleeping in record numbers; sales of alarm clocks have rocketed since the dawn chorus cut out. The carwashes that did so well are now closing their fists tightly on their record profits, as all indications for the next quarter are that business is going to drop steeply. Every time a bird flies past complete strangers clutch at each other in hope – *Look!,* they exclaim, before dropping their hand as the bird continues on, further into the sky, to wherever it is all the other birds have flown. Tracking devices have proved inconclusive, scrambled signals throwing the charts off-kilter. *It's as if they don't want us to know,* a complete stranger theorised darkly to me on the bus, while around us everyone nodded and thought about it. Pet canaries have taken to mysteriously disappearing, or to pining at the doors of their cages, another development the conspiracy theorists have grasped at. People are still leaving their birdfeeders up, even though the peanuts are starting to mould in the rain, disintegrating inside their wire holders.

I wake up to silence at 6 am and more and more it really does feel like the end of the world. The morning sounds without birdsong are half-finished, hollow. I get up straight away and turn on the television to reassure myself that things still exist, but on every channel they are talking about the birds too. *Something needs to happen,* I think, *something needs to give.* Today was the first day I saw no birds at all, though I've been keeping my eyes out, my fingers crossed. And I think more and more now about the bird that used to attack the windows of my childhood home, pecking so violently at the glass that it had to be taped, and whether it was loneliness that drove it to such reckless lengths, trying to find the bird on the other side. Or whether it was anger, or whether it was just a stupid bird who couldn't tell the difference between inside and out. It was a jackdaw, I remember. Its feathers were greying and eventually it chipped its beak, and it stopped bothering us so much. It sat for hours on the lawn and my mother threw it hard tokens of bread. *Maybe we are giving the birds too much power*, I suggest, and everyone looks at me as though I have broken a spell, their coffee cups halting in midair.

IDEAL

Oscar Schwartz

TO AN IDEAL friend,

My mum came home with a book for me a few months ago. It was the written correspondence between two famous writers. The cover was a black and white snap of the authors as young men, leaning over a book with rapt faces. I read the first few letters, but I had no time to really feel them, so I put the book back on the table. Just last weekend I picked it up again. I had planned on being active, because summer is starting and it's almost New Year's, but the cold weather is holding on. No point in getting wet. So I opened the book of letters again. I've been reading it in bed, not really thinking about anything else.

I've concluded that it's best to describe the letters as heartbreaking. This is the case for two reasons: First – the correspondence marks a narrative of two young men who are constantly imprisoning themselves by searching for real freedom. Their lives are electrifying but tragic. Second – I have some close, long-standing and unquestionably loyal friends. On balance, they are the most interesting people I've come across. The other night I was at a party. It was loud. I felt an intense connection to everyone else there. I felt myself open inwards to the whole dance floor. We were like small fish moving in and out of each other in the shallow water beneath a pier. There was a perfect moment at about 2 am when I could talk to anyone. I sat outside on the concrete with some friends, and we discussed the things we see and hear in bed before sleep. But here is my problem: as these moments pass and the tension of the party slackens, my desire for a truly open-faced relationship pushes on, but in my friends it dissolves. Walls are rebuilt. By the next morning their secret lives are once again secret, unutterably personal. This process of opening and closing has always troubled me, but never so much as when I read the letters of these writers. Every letter in the book is an act of nudity. The image that accompanied me as I read the letters was of two young men sitting naked at a small dining table, facing each other with open chests, telling their thoughts out loud. They ignore the desire to sleep. They push through the heavy waves of morning-rationality-regret. When I reached the end of their correspondence I placed the book back on the shelf, and the two young men stood up from the table, dressed and left each other. And that's when my heart broke. I have no friends to reach down into. This is why I am writing to you. I am certain that if my mother knew how the book would affect me, she would never have bought it in the first place.

I used to think that the tides keeping me from the underside of my friends' minds were the few years I spent at a different school. At my first school I only had one friend. He was taller than me and had a violent streak, which I liked.

Every Friday my friend's grandmother would pick us up and we'd spend the afternoon at her house. She was a skinny lady with watery eyes. She was not affectionate to her grandson or to me, but we enjoyed her company; she played our games with the intense vested interest of an intelligent kid, rather than the authorial detachment of an adult. The game I most enjoyed was called 'Lands'. All three of us would choose a room in the house to convert into a 'Land' of our choice. I once converted the living room into a boxing ring made out of chairs, rope and mattresses. The boy and I boxed with pillows on our hands as gloves, and his grandmother was referee. After three rounds she asked if we could swap; she wanted a shot in the ring boxing and I had to be referee. I said no because girls don't box. She was so offended that she stopped playing with us for the rest of the afternoon, and she sat reading an old gardening magazine in the green kitchen.

She would also tell us stories about her life in Russia as we ate sour cream on rye-bread toast for afternoon tea. The stories were always set on the farm where she grew up, and there were only a few recurring characters. This consistency gave her stories the timelessness of fables. One story had a particularly strong effect on me. Its imagery has followed me like a hungry seagull:

On her farm there was a lemon tree. Every spring she would climb it and pick the lemons for her mother. She fell from a high branch during one of her harvests, landing in the thorn bushes next to the tree. One of the bush's branches pierced her cheek right through. As she pulled the branch back out of her cheek the thorns caught the flesh and ripped deeper into her cheek. After a few days the cut turned black, so her parents took her to the local hospital. She shared a hospital room with a young boy who she never saw due to the curtained partition. Every day a doctor would come to check their progress, reading the nurse's charts, taking a peremptory look at his patients. Before leaving he would stand in the curtained partition between the two children's beds, hidden from view to both. He would say, 'And now, children, we test your minds; will it be heads or will it be tails?'. The young boy would quickly proffer an answer but she would stay silent. She would hear the wavering chime of the coin in the air and a slap of the palm. Without exception the doctor would congratulate the young boy for his correct guess, and without exception my friend's grandmother, then just a young girl, would shake with indignation. Her objection to the game was grounded in the fact that she couldn't see the doctor's coin flip. He had the power to fabricate the result every time. The doctor would laugh after the game and say, 'Next time, little girl, you must be quicker.' His brown shoes would then exit the way they entered.

I've never shared the story with any of my friends. I am telling you, though, because if we're going to establish the stark naked relationship I want us to have, it is an important story for you to know. I guess it has taken on some kind of biblical significance in my life. I feel this story like it's some familiar landscape I visited many times early in my life.

No doubt you have questions. I imagine that your questions are of two kinds. First – questions about the events in the story. For example, why did the doctor insist on performing such an absurd task? Second – questions about the story itself. For example, are we supposed to assume that the story is true, or is it a fiction invented by a creative, or senile, grandmother? You might find it frustrating that I offer no more information about the story, or the grandmother, or myself. I have many ideas as to what the story might mean. The last thing I want to do, however, is infect your pure interpretation of the story. I want you to write back addressing the story directly. I want your unadulterated, honest opinion. I want you to strip naked in your response, like I have just done. I expect it and I know you won't disappoint. We are kindred in that way.

But, just in case you're finding it hard to frame your thoughts around what I have just written, here are two focused questions to get you thinking in a certain direction; they may help you structure a response: First – how would you feel about participating in a game of chance in which the element of chance is annulled? Second – let's assume for a moment that the grandmother's story is fiction; would it matter? Anything worth inventing in the mind is as true as we care to make it. Our relationship depends on it.

Yours

SMOKE

Tymek Woodham

HE (UNNAMED) LOOKED out through the blinds again. To leave, or to stay. The dust of the road tempted him, as it always did. Always he studied the thin slit of the view outside, and the buildings blocking out what lay ahead. Smoke and sand rose over Baghdad. The day had waned. 7.45 p.m. Al-Ghadir district.

There were 1.3 million Christians living in Iraq in 2003. By recent counts, it has fallen to something more like 500,000.

FATHER MEYASSR AL-QASPOTROS: *[looks towards the camera]* I just wonder, when does this ignorance end? When does this bigotry end? When is there an end to weak-minded people not treating or thinking of other people as a human?

The old man steps away from the window. Christmas came and went without any trouble. When was the last time they showed their decorations for the streets outside to see? He turned to face the window again. The road can take you places – or it can bring the violence to you.

He leaves the kitchen. Walking through the door, he sees sitting around the table his wife and three brothers drinking tea. Politics. How can you speak of such things now? His brother's voice is rising. The man felt an unmistakable urge to silence him. Every night. Every night they do this now. It has no end.

Words as thick as smoke.

Political uncertainty continues to grow in Iraq, a er 35 m rs of the State of Law coali essed a desire t refuse any that brings allegiance with f ime-minister Dr. Iyad Alli. between coalition have be developing since the 'out-going' pri e-minister Nouri Maliki insisted on re-nomination for a second term. Anonymous sourcing from within the political establishment revealed that the first sign exposing these differences of opinion was the resignation Abdullah, former dir tor the prime-minister's off e

In spite of the 2010 March agreement between the State of Law Coalition and the Iraqi National Movement, fear is still resonating within the heart of the embryonic democracy; that neither side is moving closer to an agreement about the next stage for Iraq. In a re nt statement, rmer pri -mi Iyad Allawi lared th sect- Allawi,

Outskirts of Baghdad. The newspaper curled in the flames until words became smoke, the smoke became vapour, and vapour the sky. The men abandoned their fire, rifles in hand.

MR. YOUNADIM YOUSIF: *[gravely]* The government bears full responsibility for these attacks, because they already promised to secure the Christians.

FATHER MEYASSR AL-QASPOTROS: *[resolute, but weak]* Yes, we are threatened, but we will not stop praying. We do not want to leave the country because we will leave an empty space. Be careful not to hate the ones killing us because they know not what they are doing. God forgive them.

(Do you know what happens to a home-made time-fused fragmentation grenade when its fuse runs out? Its insides explode, sending out thousands of tiny projectiles at almost incalculable speeds: flechettes, tiny darts that slit the air; notched wire; ball bearings; even the fragments of the casing turn into shards of murder. Within a 15m radius, you're wounded. How bad depends on the grenade. 5m and you're dead. The individual pieces of shrapnel hit with such a collective force, whole limbs can be severed from their bodies. Especially if the maker has improvised: mixing further explosives with the projectiles.)

A window smashed. Two grenades fell. It had happened. The man kicked the closest one as far as he could into the other room, and flung himself to close the door. His wife had ducked behind the table, overturned in the panic. One of the brothers lunged to grasp the grenade; to throw it back out of the window.

They detonated almost simultaneously, before the man could close the door; before the friend could lob it back. The shrapnel erupted and the furniture near the blasts collapsed as the weak structure of the house trembled from the explosions. With two dead and three barely living, the smoke cleared slowly around their eyes.

Yet more Christians flee the country, forging the biggest exodus Iraq has ever seen across the borders to Kurdistan, Syria, Turkey and Jordan in- fatalities in Al-Ghadir only scratch the surface. Estimates of 1000 have left since the attack earlier this year, when, at 17.00 on the 31st of October

Opposite *Our Lady of Salvation* Cathedral, two guards standing outside the Iraq Stock Exchange look up too late, and are shot.

They've broken down the doors. Shot the lights. The congregation scatters to the floor, amidst the dust, hiding behind the pews that cannot shield them.

UNNAMED (MALE): They came to kill Iraq, not Iraqis.

In the bare, flickering candlelight of the hall, Father Sahib stands as a ghost – facing the men who run towards him and, clutching his crucifix, he pleads with them to spare the worshippers. He was flung to the floor and shot.

'Allahu akbar.' Words as thick as smoke rise through the dusty hall. They open fire.

Those that lie around Dr Thanna Nassir are beyond help. He covers his ears, hearing, with every bomb and every shot, people dying. Any bomb, any shot might kill him, and he will hear them no more. Four hours pass – silence, then gunfire, silence, then gunfire.

[enter REPORTER and CAMERAMAN into the hospital. By the bed, UNNAMED (FEMALE) is hysterical]

UNNAMED (FEMALE): What can I say? The father and son were killed in the attack. They were killed while they lay on the ground pretending to be dead. But they were killed when the gunmen threw grenades and exploded their explosive belts. What can I say?

The men hear forces shouting from outside. They have come to kill them, but it is too late. He smiled. They cannot follow me where I am going. He tugged on his belt.

  - How is it?
    - Bad.
  - How many have been killed?
    - Nobody knows. They've only released the estimates.
  - How many?
    - Over 50.
  - Wounded?

- Almost all.
- Are you OK?

RADI CLIMIS: *[holding his blood-soaked head-bandage]* If we didn't love this country, we wouldn't have stayed here.

FATHER MEYASSR AL-QASPOTROS: We must die here. We can't leave this country.

STEPHEN KAROMI: Everyone wants to leave for one reason: to protect ourselves and keep our sanity.

As if the blood were rain: red dapples across the corner of the hall in thin, splattered droplets beside the scorch marks. Abandoned coats and shoes and wayward fabrics pile up, some flushed red, others fading with coats of dust and rubble. A priest's stole is woven around the shattered remnants of a pew; the black material hides the blood until it leaks through the edges of the white cross stitched in the centre. Beside the death pile, two decorative roses are crushed and blackened beside what could be scorch marks – perhaps the flesh strung off by the impact. The photographer bends to take his photo.

FALLAH: *[shouting, desperate]* If they want us to leave, we will leave – and if they want us to sleep on the street, we will sleep on the street! If they want us to join them and be terrorists – we will do! Just let us live.

All across the dry land, some leave and some stay. The incense lingers in the air, but is uncertain. In the evening, many more Christians will look through the blinds at the dust on the road, watching it sift across the ground, and wonder if the words of commitment to a free world will stop the real world from shattering their windows, arcing inside their room, waiting for detonation. In the evening, words as thick as smoke plume over the charred houses; through the scaffolding on the beaten church; away across the borders; through whole countries; landing far, far away, as if the fire never burned.

Spoken word excerpts in *Smoke* are taken from the following sources:

Leland, John & Omar Al-Jawoshy. Middle East: Christians are Casualties of 10 Baghdad Attacks. December 30 2010. The New York Times. <http://tinyurl.com/6awsjtd>

Leland, John. Iraqi Christians Lie Low on Christmas. December 24th 2010. Assyrian International News Agency. <http://tinyurl.com/66y2bey>

Adnan, Duraid. Middle East: Church Attack Seen as Strike at Iraq's Core. November 1st 2010. The New York Times. <http://tinyurl.com/6fput6q>

Yahoo News: <http://tinyurl.com/6h588q3> (Content no longer available)

You've made the alarm clock cry

Peter Dawncy

NOW YOU'RE A dripping tap. I wonder whether that's of some significance? You stare straight at me, dripping consistently. Is that the beginnings of a smile I see?

But it's too late, for I've already become a puddle, my question expressed as ripples in which stars undulate. And now you're a paper boat! It's rude to float on people like that you know. Imagine if I floated all over you: you'd be furious! You'd beach me immediately – no doubt about it. Are you enjoying bobbing through the mid-month moon in my belly? I suppose you can anchor there if you'd like. I won't say no.

Where are you going? It's as though you've been swept onto a freak breeze, yet I can see the wings that work to carry you further from me. I wish more than anything that I could follow. You seem so beautiful streaming into the clouds.

I am following! How did that happen? My wings are pretty sleek too. Where now? Higher? Can we find a high bough on which to perch and talk out this lingering night? We'll watch the world below as we exchange our secrets.

But no: no high places, no exchanging of secrets. Instead it's down a chimney and into a room in which a man sits watching the rain. Where are you in this typical scene? It's getting cold in here without you. Really cold. I know I worry too much and ask a lot of questions, and say some silly things, but when you're around I'm comforted. My days of worry are behind me though, and I won't ask or even say anything more. My lips are tightly sealed, I promise. See? Please, I don't like being like this.

Now you've made the alarm clock cry: she splutters sobs between her tick-tocks. And the pot plant, his leaves quivering in great wrenching gasps. Then the coat hanger on the door swings and sprinkles tears over the walls.

And who's going to clean this up? I ask, as I wipe away my own tears.

FOX

Peter Dawncy

NO ONE ELSE knows the fox that sits in the scrub by my back gate. When I'm alone I'll give him the compost and meat scraps, and occasionally, if he's polite, I'll whisper to him as I tickle his whiskers and chin – tell him he's a good fox, a clever fox, a pretty fox. I wish I would stop mistaking his wild calls for the neighbours though – he'll think I'm just making excuses to see him.

Now he's playing with the children and nipping off fingers. He drops the pink nubs into my lap and sits, growls softly, back arrow-straight, eyes gleaming (I notice his tongue is much thinner than I'd thought).

Hush – I touch a finger to his nose and fetch him a rabbit liver. The way he walks off startles me, and I never have time to blink and turn away.

Of course I can't help but take him to bed on the colder nights of winter. His coat is so homely; I don't even need sheets; I disappear altogether beneath his bristly rustic redness, his tongue, twinkling in the darkness. In my dreams I pray he'll be gone when I wake.

SHIPS

Peter Dawncy

A WOMAN WITH chestnut tresses is twinkling her fingers beside her ears. Now she's darting out a hand and tugging a loose thread on my sleeve. Now both hands are twinkling again. Now she's tugging again, now twinkling, now tugging, now twinkling, tugging, twinkling, tugging, twinkling…

Each time she tugs, the thread emerges a little further; it looks so insignificant, coiled as it is, asleep on my knee. Now she's tugging again. Twinkling, tugging, twinkling…

It's as though she knows something I don't. Yet I know that when the thread ends, my secrets will crash from my brow, like a wave, I suppose. And I also know that she already knows most, probably all, or has at least guessed them, and knows that I know she knows. Yet still she tugs and twinkles, tugs and twinkles, tugs and twinkles, her anticipation brimming in her shining eyes.

Perhaps she just likes the coolness foaming over her in the calm of a clear night, forming puddles in the dips of her shoulders, settling, harbouring the wayward ships that chance upon her in the dark.

POSTSCRIPT

Michaela Atienza

1

THERE IS NOTHING unusual about a man sitting in a library, unless the library is the last one standing in a four hundred-mile radius, and the man is forty-one and learning how to read.

The windows have been painted an impenetrable black. The only light coming in is sunlight streaming down through a hole in the ceiling and onto a mess of broken spines and mottled pages. In this section of the library, the few books that have remained whole lie face down like dead things.

But the man has managed to rescue one. He sits cross-legged underneath the gaping ceiling and struggles with the sounds that make up the word 'oxygen', his nose only a few inches away from the faded pages.

It starts to rain, and the water comes right into the library. The man takes out his umbrella.

2

It's always raining down in the archives, even if it's not raining outside. Weak halogen lamps flicker as if they know they are about to die. Something thick and green oozes out of the pipes and onto the books, making the pages stick together.

Marta stands on tiptoe, straining to reach a large, orange volume on a shelf just out of reach. Five or six other books lie open at her feet, all photographic spreads – an albatross in flight, an elephant on its hind legs, the circus master gesturing to the delighted crowd, a rocket ship, its base obscured by smoke and fire. But none of these are enough for Marta, who has learned that the larger the book, the better the pictures.

She hears laughter a few shelves away and frowns, knowing it's the boy from yesterday who came and tried to take her spot underneath the bright lamp. She threw a book in his face and watched him run away.

Marta doesn't like knowing she isn't the only one sneaking around down in the archives.

She is about to give up on the book, when someone reaches up, pries it out of the shelf and hands it to her. She turns to find the boy from yesterday smiling – the bruise starting to darken on his temple – and offering the book to her as a gesture of truce.

3

Pep opens the dictionary and finds that someone has taken all the vowels.

Whole sections have been removed and the left-over pages are full of tiny rectangular holes. They have been meticulously cut; their edges are perfectly straight. One entry reads:

v n· r· ·bl dj \□v -n r(-)-b l,□v n-r -b l

1: *d crd sp c y by r g s rh st r c l s c t n*

   2: *c ng f h p ct hr gh g , ch ct r̦, n tt nm nts < v n r bl j zz m s*

c n>; c v y n g n mp n f g d g dn s nd b n v l n c

Pep can see the holes in page seventy-nine through the holes in page seventy-seven.

He picks up the book beside the dictionary and finds that it has been completely stripped, just fringes now, jagged between the worn backing and a front cover that reads LICE IN W ND L ND. The girl in the picture, standing tall with a large hole where her head should be, has suffered an even greater loss.

The next book Pep picks up contains only k's and b's. He looks around, more out of habit than anything else. Pep empties the book, tearing out what remains of the pages and stuffing the scraps into his pocket.

4

Benny sits at his desk, making words.

He used to be a thief, back when what he stole had value. Now he's just a scrounger with a pair of scissors and a pot of glue. The pot of glue sits on his desk. It used to be a jar of olives. Now it is filled with a sticky amber substance that has spilled over the rim and is oozing down the sides, the shiny stuff catching what light there is and gathering in a thick pool around the bottom. Benny has saved the toothpick that he used to eat the olives – one end for his teeth and the other for the glue.

Benny still knows how to read and write. He can make most of the sounds he is thinking, he can match the sounds to letters, and he can assemble the letters into crude, lopsided words.

He leans over his work, holding his breath as he puts the letters down in sequence before turning them over with his little finger, blank side up, one by one. Every few seconds, he exhales and stirs the scraps.

5

At about six in the evening, Billy comes in through the library's main entrance with a suitcase. It's about half his size and as he drags it behind him it leaves a wide track in the dust. Far above him are the rusted blades of ceiling fans that haven't turned in years.

He comes up to three doors. A sign over the first reads GOAL – GOUT, the second reads KNOR – KRIS, and the third reads simply DISPATCH.

Billy opens the first door and disappears into the dark emerging about two hours later, still dragging his suitcase, which is much heavier.

6

Joe sits by his father's bed, the evening hot against his skin. The lights are out, but Joe can see his father's torso tucked away beneath the smooth white sheets. He can see the weak outline of an IV bottle, the tubing wrapped around the stand and running right into Joe's father's hand. There's a needle in a vein, Joe knows, hidden somewhere in the wrinkles. The plastic looks stiff and strange against all that skin, hanging loose around the bones.

Joe's father's eyes are shut. He could be dreaming. The monitor beside him beeps every few seconds; Joe tries not to look at the line running jagged across the screen.

Joe's father begins a story in the dark. 'A beggar comes in through, through the gates carrying a sack…'

7

Celia stands across the street, out of breath and dripping sweat and rainwater. She stares at the seven stories of concrete, all the way up and all the way down. Her fist is clenched; her fingers are closed around something sacred. She's afraid to find that what she's written there has been lost, washed out in the downpour.

She backs into the doorway opposite the library. She presses her hand to her skirt and then takes a look inside it. What is left of the word is leaking blue into the grooves of her palm. It now reads, *ber…* . She shuts her eyes and tries to recall the rest. She remembers only how it looked. She remembers how the thick red lines were blotted at the edges, how they came together in strange ways. Celia stares at the wall, hoping it will yield an answer. The wall is a smooth blind white.

She takes another look at her palm. Then she walks back up toward the main road, away from the library, her arms dangling at her sides.

8

Benny takes his time untying the knot on a plastic bag. Inside are a hundred and eighty-seven v's which he found in a book in the library. They're a prize; the edges are perfectly straight and they're all the same size.

Benny was always careful about taking letters out of books. He would cut them out one by one, slip them into little plastic bags, and replace the books on the shelves when he was done. He wasn't like the careless thieves who tore whole pages out, although he couldn't blame them. He liked the idea of being able to come back to the library knowing that the book would still be there.

Benny used to marvel at the weight of books in general. He would try to guess how many words each one contained. He used to wonder what would happen if he had more words in his head than he could manage to get down.

He finally gets the bag open and digs through the pile of letters at the bottom. Some cling to the plastic or are caught in the folds. He selects a V, fat, tilted, and wrinkled on the paper, and reties the knot on the bag. Benny used to wonder about people who refused to steal, people who had words they couldn't afford to write down.

9

'A beggar comes in, in through, in through, in through the gates carrying a sack, asks to see the rich man... the richest man in the city'. There's something caught in the gears of the story, something solid, sticky – phlegm, maybe, or spit. The words feel rough, regurgitated. They rasp and stumble out as if they are being spoken for the first time. But the story is whole and intact; Joe's father knows it by heart. 'The beggar makes his way, to the rich man's home his rags trail, trailing behind him as he winds his way through the streets drag, dragging his sack over the... over those cobblestones... those cobblestones...'

10

Sonny is sitting on the low wall in front of the library, carving figures into the stone with a knife. WHY, he scrawls, without understanding. He drags the blade up and down and across the surface with ease; the lines are perfectly straight.

He leaves out what he thinks is the last letter, which he has seen but cannot reproduce with a knife on stone. Not without some difficulty. The rest of WHY, to him, is beautiful and looks good on a wall.

11

The benches are long and narrow. They are warped in some places, but they are still arranged in rows. Ellen sits up front, in the middle of the bench nearest the counters. Her feet are flat on the floor, wet inside wet shoes. She empties her pockets and places the contents on the aging wood: some coins, a lighter, a pen.

She picks up the pen and begins to dismantle it, unscrewing the midsection, pulling the two halves apart, removing the inner cartridge. The faded lettering on the top half reads only *NC*. Dangling from the bottom half is a broken, blackened chain.

Ellen puts the two empty shells away. The chain hangs out of her pocket and the links trail in the dust.

She takes the lighter, clicks it, and watches the flame glance over the tip of the inner shaft. She does this patiently, carefully. The clock above the counter reads 12:02. It is four in the afternoon.

Ellen puts the lighter out. She presses the tip of the pen against her finger, but the ink sits still and dark inside its plastic casing. She tries it on the bench. Still nothing. Frustrated, she presses harder and harder until she scores a deep, dry cut in the wood.

12

Benny stares at his nearly finished word. He is particularly proud of the latter half – an R on cloth, an S on newsprint, a T and half of some other letter on a piece of cardboard.

The R is a weak and washed out red, the S is almost lost in a smudge of ink, the T has been scrawled out with something thin and broken that has sliced right through the paper, leaving a gash where the vertical line should be. The black from the newsprint is coming off on Benny's fingers. There comes a point, he used to say, when print won't stay on paper anymore. Letters weren't cheap back then, so something else had to be.

Lamplight seeps in through a broken window near the desk as Benny studies the gap in the word.

He has all the consonants, but is missing three of the vowels and is nursing a depleted supply of the other two. *Who needs them*, he used to tell himself. But he keeps the vowels in their boxes and tries not to use them.

13

A seventy-five-year-old woman shivers in the doorway and waits for the rain to stop. Her groceries are on the floor next to her. The bags are soaking up the water. She's forgotten her umbrella, and doesn't know how she's going to get home. She is struck by a plaque set into the wall. Rust has eaten away at the words.

...thanks the kind sup...
...with warm con...
...tional Lib...

She vaguely remembers 'warm' and 'kind', but can't quite place them. When she turns around, she realises that this is the entrance to the library and that she has been here before. Many times, a long, long time ago. Paint is coming off the door. The woman notices it is slightly open, just as the rain lets up.

14

Benny climbs onto his chair. It creaks under his weight. He reaches into the shelf and takes down several boxes and jars. He scours the corners, up to his elbows in a much deeper darkness, the dust fine in some places and crusty in others. He feels around until he finds an old cigarette container. It doesn't make a sound as he brings it into the weak light of the room; it's quiet even as he shakes it. He flips the lid open and peeks inside. A yellow scrap of paper lies at the bottom. It is Benny's last O.

He stands on the chair holding the open container, and doesn't move.

15

Joe inches closer. His father is still stumbling over 'cobblestones'.

The story is being called up from a dark corner somewhere, where it has been waiting for decades, like a toy that has died in its box, rusty and lock-jawed, its joints brittle even though they have never been used.

The story has never been used. It comes up wrong, doesn't fit in the mouth. Joe's father is gagging on the words. 'Through' sounds like a ragged last breath, like dry consonants scraping against each other. Joe bends over to adjust his father's pillow. The fan standing in the corner creaks as it turns on its base. The blades send the heat reeling.

Joe is close enough to hear his father wheezing. The air comes up cold and dry, tearing at the lungs and the throat. Every breath has been wrought into telling this story. 'The rich man, throws a fit. The rich man... orders the begging man... to leave he laughs, he laughs, he *laughs!*'

The last 'laughs' is violent. Joe's father spits it out like he is spitting out bits of barbed wire. The choice has come down to speaking or breathing, and Joe's father has chosen to speak. 'The beggar, laughs all the way to the door.' Joe puts his hand next to his father's. He can feel the sheets move slightly in the pauses between words.

16

Benny's chair wobbles beneath his feet.

He used to say that the C.O.L. was overcharging for vowels. As the most expensive letters, they were first to go. *Who needs them*, Benny told himself the first time he discovered that he didn't have enough to write his mother. He spent the money on the cheaper consonants and sent the letter off, hoping she would be able to imagine what was missing. Benny tried to convince himself that vowels were just a way to say nothing, the written sound of air, or emptiness.

But right now, as he stands on the chair, staring at the letter lying at the bottom of the near-empty cigarette container, Benny knows. He's not likely to find another O.

Benny shakes the box. *Who needs them*, he tries to remember. *Who needs them*. The O flutters out and lands right side up in the center of his hand. He jumps down.

Benny completes the word and looks up for the first time, staring at the cracked window, rain caught on the glass, the floor beneath speckled in shadow.

17

Celia stops at the corner, where the main road and the loop intersect. She studies the pedestrian sign. The figure of the man in red is flickering, disappearing and appearing again and again. The man in red is turning into the man in green. The flickering continues. The green is turning green. The flickering is getting faster. The man is being emptied of his insides and his outline is becoming shrill. The man is now the bright green shell of a man.

Celia looks up and down the road, across the intersection, and as far into the loop as she can manage. There's no one around. She can't hear sirens or footsteps. Not even a car has come speeding down the street in the last few minutes. The sign must be broken.

Dark spots are forming on the pavement. Celia's first instinct is to clench her fist and put her hand back in her pocket to protect the *ber...*

The sign has turned red again – a bright red outline flashing frantically, disappearing and appearing around nothing. Celia turns around and heads back toward the library. The street remains empty behind her; the sign is definitely broken.

18

The story is winding down to an even weaker whisper. 'Everyone forgets. Everyone forgets the beggar... the beggar ever asked... to see the rich man, no one ever asked... the beggar why...'

Joe leans forward, eyes peeled. The fan has stalled. The air, moving in a steady current now, pushes the door open. A thin shaft of light cuts at the dark. Joe takes his father's hand. He wants to ask his father to continue. He wants to hear more.

There used to be a way to say and ask and tell his father all the things he's thinking, but Joe is at a loss for them now. Instead he sits in the dark, and listens to the beeping, and waits.

THE SCRATCH

Camille Eckhaus

SHE'S COME HOME and he is happy to see her. He is happy to see her and he is not happy to see her. There is a scratch on the back of her left hand. A long line the colour of a dried riverbed. It runs from the corner of her wrist to the base of her thumb. *Lunate* to *Trapezoid*. *Trapezoid* to *Lunate*. He stares but he can't tell which way it goes. It wasn't there when she left. Looking at it makes him cold. Makes his skin shiver. He stares and it doesn't go away. There is her and then there is the scratch.

Before she went away she used to bite the skin around her nails. They would bleed and the earth brown blood would stain the beds of her cuticles. He would take her hand and kiss the torn skin and she'd sigh and pull away. 'Leave me be,' she would say, voice framed in irritation: the centre distant. His pain would be white-hot and her dismissal would thrum through him for days until she smiled again. Smiled just at him again. Then he would be full of light. She'd always come and gone from him like a tide.

Now that she has come back her hands are clean and there's a ladder in her tights but then she's always ruining them. Her hair is longer but that's how it goes. This is what happens as her body is pulled through one moment into another. It's to be expected.

There is just that scratch on her hand that makes him feel naked on a winter's night. This is unexpected, sudden. Part of her is absent.

They are in the car and he is driving and he asks where she got it. She shrugs. 'I don't remember,' she says and her voice is slinking away. He tries to pull it back with his own.

Later that night she is asleep beside him. Turned away from him, sleeping as she always does on her side. The curve of her spine is the same. Alabaster in night time shadows. He is not asleep. He is thinking. That scratch. The word an edged echo in his mind. That scratch from an unknown place. From contact with something real, something she touched whilst she was away. That touched her. Her skin ripped through and she says she doesn't remember how. It would have hurt. She should remember. She is holding a lie.

He is not asleep but he is lying on his back and staring at the ceiling and he is thinking. He is thinking about that scratch but he does not know what he thinks. Only that he is scared.

'About that scratch,' he says to her the next morning. He has arranged the condiment jars in line in front of him. A rag-tag battalion standing at attention between his frontline and hers. She looks at him over her coffee cup like she doesn't understand. Reaches for the sugar and punches a hole in his defence. He finds he doesn't know how to finish the sentence. So he doesn't.

Eventually the scratch fades. It fades and it doesn't.

WHEN THE GOLDFISH DIE

Peter Donaldson

'WHAT DO I think of memory? I don't know. Maybe it's a tyrant. People say goldfish only have a five-second memory. Wishful thinking. They want to believe that so they don't feel so bad about locking them up in empty cells. These days the scientists seem to think they have a memory span of over three months. Three months. That's a long time to look at the same fake pebbles and bit of fake grass… Yes, I'll have another scotch thanks. No, straight. No no, my shout this time. I don't know how you can drink that bathwater, but cheers. Your wife might be turning up soon you say? No, you don't have to worry about mine appearing anytime, that's for sure… Anyway where was I… Ah yes, so a few days ago, my neighbours jetted off to India to see their daughter or cousin or something, and they left me their goldfish. In a very small tank. Nothing in it but hideously bright-coloured little rocks and an artificial rush covered in scum. And three fish. I named them Big, Whitey and Little. Anyway I tried to feed them just as my neighbours had told me to, but Whitey ate most of what I put in there. Big got a bit, but Little got hardly any. Whitey started to annoy me. I didn't want to overfeed them but no matter how much I put in there or where I put it, Whitey would fight the others off. He was quite aggressive. Even between feeding times, Whitey would be bothersome, just pecking and sucking at the others willy-nilly, particularly Little. I didn't realise how much this was getting to me until the next day at work, when my concentration was all over the place. All I could think of was poor little Little getting pecked at. I thought about what I might do. I even entertained the idea of implementing a behaviour management plan, of maybe belting Whitey with a chopstick every time he attacked Big or Little. Of course this was a crazy idea, and I don't have the time or patience anyway. It came to a head that night when I got home. I went straight to the tank, and at a quick glance I could see that Little had only one eye. I felt the blood beat big in my head; Whitey the bastard. I could have picked him out of the tank and thrown him against the wall. I didn't though. You know those flexible steel colander things you put in saucepans for steaming? I grabbed one of those from the kitchen and trapped him in it. He hates it and so do I. At times I feel a bit authoritarian or a bit overprotective maybe. Sometimes you probably should just let things be and let things live; let them live or die. Feeding Whitey is hard. I have to wet up the little fish balls and then try to jam them through the little holes in the colander before they float back up to the top. You know what that fish food is made of? Fish. No wonder they resort so quickly to cannibalism… Yep, I'll have another scotch; you can keep your mouse-piss… Your wife is just dropping off the kids then popping in you say? She trusts you, doesn't she?… Ah yes, Little. He's close to dead now I think. Cuts a haunting figure though, the poor little bugger. And docile. Just does slow laps around the top of Whitey's cage, lopsided like a one-legged sentry, with one big eye and one empty socket. You can pretty much see straight through his head. Bits of bone and blood everywhere. Makes you nauseous. Some kind of fungus seems to be working away at him too, trailing around solemnly after him like a toddler's favourite threadbare blankie. It doesn't look like he has much to live for anymore. Have you ever heard of Beryl Markham? No? Good then I can tell you anything. If I remember correctly she was a British-Kenyan aviatrix born early last century. She was wild. Rebellious. Adventurous. First woman to cross the Atlantic solo, first non-stop flight from England to North America. Married ten times or something, hundreds of lovers; noblemen, writers. Didn't they *live* back then! Anyway she wrote a memoir called *West with the Night*. Sold pretty poorly I think, but Hemingway thought her writing put his to shame. I'll bet he could drink her under the table though. And maybe one of her writer boyfriends wrote the book for her, who really knows?… Sorry, yes, the point is that in the memoir she said 'Life is life and fun is fun, but it's all so quiet when the goldfish die.'

I can't remember what she was talking about, but that one line has stayed with me, and it's all I can think about lately. What do you think she meant? I'll tell you what I think…is this your wife? Very pleased to meet you, I must apologise, I've just been chewing your husband's ear off and he's probably sick to death of it… no, no but can I share one more thing with you both before you head off to dinner? You look lovely by the way and I hope he cherishes you… Anyway it's a dream I had last night, I'd love to know what you make of it… I'm swimming in deep murky water. I can see a small distance ahead of me though, and I don't seem to need to breathe. I'm not sure how I got here. Suddenly I come across a metallic glint, and realise there is a deep-sea cage. As I peek in through the cracks some scattered spots of light pass over a figure. It quickly comes closer and I move back. It peers out at me. It has one eye and one gaping socket, from which grey entrails hang suspended like feelers. I notice she is rotting, and somehow know she is my wife, or what my wife once was. Something comes over me and I grab her throat through a crack in the cage. Her neck feels like a bar of over-soaked soap as I squeeze, and her one eye bulges till it fades… Next thing I know I'm on the inside of the cage. Don't remember how I got here. She isn't anywhere. I don't feel anything in particular. I sort of don't want to be here. I move around the cage and notice that I could probably just fit through one of the cracks. I don't go though. I sit on a rock and stay as the dark earthy water swirls around me. I stay! What the hell do you think that means? Ah don't worry about me, be on your way and have a good night. I think I might know. Whatever you do, cradle your goldfish with open hands.'

Four Pairs of Marco Polo

Tori Truslow

YOU SHOULD NOT be able to lose a thirty-acre field in such a well-spaced city. Downtown, perhaps, where the hotels and office-blocks sweep everything else out of sight; not here in the old town, with its broad roads and white-walled temple compounds. But walking up Na Phra Lan Road, looking to my left – I can't see it. According to the glossy screen of my phone, I should be looking at:

Sanam Luang, a long grassy shadow to the Palace. It served as a Royal cremation ground, a site for festivals, and even a rice field, a siege-defying source of plenty in the heart of the Old City. The annual Ploughing Ceremony is still held here, as is a kite-flying festival. Just as it provided respite in ancient times of hardship, it can do the same for you in your Rattanakosin walk. Pause here and picture a time when it was an oasis of dancing rice stalks in a city of gold.

I would. But there's just road, pavement, streetlamps, vendors, trees, pigeons. So much for respite.

'Hello!' calls a helpful tout, 'Grand Palace?' I shake my head and ask after the vanished field. He laughs at me, points across the road. Beyond the kerb, the trees, the fizzy-drinks stall, there's a stretch of blank concrete space, the kind my eyes are used to editing out. But I can see it now: long, empty, paved over. The field is cement steeped in afternoon heat, guarded by an old woman who sells seeds next to the 'DO NOT FEED THE PIGEONS' sign.

On my phone is a guide – the 'Secrets of Rattanakosin'. *Old Bangkok is more than just Khao San Road and the Grand Palace,* it admonishes. *Stroll the streets and discover forgotten fragments of the city's fascinating history.* The writer seems two-voiced: one on the surface, nothing more than rehashed travel copy; one waiting below, wanting to take my hand and show me hidden things. I found the article yesterday, sitting in my hotel room, trawling second-rate tourist sites – there are so many of them, so many walking tours to choose from, each sounding like a chopped and scrambled version of the last. But this was the one. I was almost, almost certain when I found it. The one that sounded most like her.

Sweat snags in my eyebrows. I wipe at it and stare across the street, watch the paving start to waver as if the field described in the article, the one where grass still grows, is about to push through. But it's only heat haze. How long since it was green here? Of course, the writer of the article can't tell me. This is a Chinese whisper city. Any poor sod trying to navigate it on the authority of these pages has one foot on the real street, the other in a neverland cobbled together from Wikitravel and Google Maps. Guides created by hacks who've never been here. I'm walking a mistranslated route, watching two fields vie in my view: the one I can really see, and the emerald-turfed burning ground of kings. I think about sending her a postcard. *Took one of your tours today. Guess what: they paved paradise.*

But I don't know where she lives these days.

Lak Muang: The City Pillar. This one is where it should be, but looks nothing like a pillar – it's a shrine, busy with attendees and waxy smoke. *The pillar, driven into the earth to mark the city's founding, is said to house Phra Lak Muang, the guardian spirit of Bangkok.* Inside, she says – besides this *genius loci* – there's a hidden horoscope for the city. *Inscribed on a bar of gold, this is both the city's birth certificate and a forecast for its future.*

What does a city want with a birth certificate? To prove it really was born *here*? I want to ask her, see her roll her eyes. *Well of course,* she would say. *Otherwise you've only got the word of history books, politicians, maps – and god knows you can't trust those.*

The last time I saw her was five, maybe six, years ago. She was folded over her laptop in a dark café, sipping a cold cup of tea, Make Poverty History band too big on her thin wrist. 'Articles for travel sites,' she said, when I asked her what she was writing. 'It's not selling out.' I shrugged off the pre-emptive defensiveness and pointed out that she'd never really travelled. 'You don't need to,' she said. 'You just do some research and write about the sights, put in some keywords. It's not for real people anyway. Rich knobs who want to do their token bit of culture between their shopping jollies and champagne jacuzzis.' She paused a moment, then: 'Sorry.'

I didn't rise to it, just ordered a latte for me and a fresh pot of jasmine for her. The place was painfully quirky, furnished with mismatched tables and flea-market lamps. Only two other tables were occupied, one by a young couple and the other by a student reading and mumbling along to the Alanis Morissette album that was playing. We sat in silence for a while. She asked – I guess it was the obvious route for the rickety conversation to take – about work; perhaps I took a bit of savage pleasure in talking about my new clients and the international golf tourney I was off to next week. She used to rant at me when I did that, but this time she just gave me a sour, weary look. I would almost have preferred the anger. She had not put her laptop away the whole time I'd been there, and now she glanced at it, shook her head, hit a couple of keys. Our drinks came. I changed track, asked if she was still writing her stories.

'Not right now. I mean, I would be, but you can't pay the bills with them. I don't even have time, you don't want to know how many freelance gigs I've got going.' She paused to tap out another sentence, frowning at the screen, before continuing. 'But this kind of crap lets me have – you know, *money and a room of my own*. I'll get back to fiction soon.'

I drank my coffee, which was awful, waiting to see if she would say anything about Mum. But she didn't, and I wouldn't know where to start.

We hugged awkwardly, just before I left. She smelled like a temple, sickly with incense.

The city moat, Klong Lod, it's called, lies long and stagnant in front of me. Her words, pooled in the palm of my hand, are once again more appealing than the reality. *Walk along the shady banks of this ancient canal, where every bridge tells a story.* The bridges are grubby white plaster, the water an oily evening glare, the warm shade no relief. Would she even have liked it here? I can't help but wonder what she would make of it. The ear-itching noise, the air with its simmering stock of petrol and grilled fat. The cable-thin man balancing on a water pipe just below the bridge, fishing with a bit of old wire. *The canal is a scratch on the surface of modern Bangkok,* she says. *Walking beside it conjures visions of a time when there were no roads.* She's an unwitting comedian. The canal is flanked by two heavy, hot roads, impossible to forget for even a moment as tuk-tuks gurgle by and their drivers shout to ask where I'm going. But in her city these things, and these people, are invisible.

In a time before boutique hotels, *this canal was both a boundary and a vein of transport and commerce.* 'Boutique hotels' is underlined and blue, linking me to a hotel booking agency. I laugh; I have to. Just as she'd laugh to think of me flying Business Class to places we never thought we'd see, and – after the meetings, after the bars and the hotel rooms – turning to these sham guides infested with glaring blue hyperlinks, looking for ones that might have been written by her. Her life and longings, scattered through a thousand faceless slabs of badly-disguised advertising.

I imagine her sifting the net, quietly snipping pieces from a dozen or so blogs by people who do know the city, who know it to the bone, who hold its secrets up to the world as if to say, see, my town, it's not all veneer, it's got a pulse and a history and a sackful of adventures waiting to be had. And she, the girl who won't fly because of the carbon footprint, took these acts of devotion and synthesised this article about a place she'd never seen, to increase some corporate website's Google rank, to earn herself enough to see out the week. I can see her biting her lip as she did it, muttering acid things about the buttery bastards who'd be reading the article and clicking the links and jetting to Bangkok.

I put my fingers to the screen, trace words that were her favourites: nook, corner, meander. I think of the millions of eyes that scan her words without ever wondering about the person who wrote them. The people who would confuse her reproduction city with the real one, trust the advice of a never-been because the unknown is such a fickle thing. Trust her, but not see her in the text. And yet the strangest thing is the way she's all over the text. Behind the tourist-guide patter I can see her yearning, to be sitting by the water with the tropical sun dying on her face. And her scorn, of course, and her hope, the endless hope that she might turn someone, anyone, away from their chandelier nights and towards an adventure, and in doing so make her dream-city real. And, perhaps, absolve herself from the sin of stealing scraps of other people's hearts. She tells her readers to get lost – turn corners on a whim and stumble upon treasures – and I'm pretty sure. Whim and stumble. They sound like clichés but they're more of her favourites. I see how her words linger on the canal and I know. It could be no one else.

I remember her making up stories, about cities on the moon or in hot jungly places, always held together by webs of canals. She would sit and summon up faraway worlds, taking parts from her head, parts from books and TV. They fascinated me when I was very small; later I got annoyed at the borrowed parts. It felt like she'd been cheating all along. But when I accused her of copying from somewhere else, all I got was a telling-off from Mum. Now, all these years later, I glimpse her worlds again, places I'd forgotten until these words shivered their surfaces.

I could never let on as I got older, of course, because she was a pain in the arse and I was too cool to care, but there was something about those stories. Not that it matters now. I don't think she's written one in years. She never mentioned them in those last petering-out phone conversations. But they carry on in these echoes, and I chase them like a child in a never-ending game.

The walk along the canal is long, and the dusk brings no relief – in fact, the lower the sun gets, the thicker the humidity seems to swell. It's a long way back to my air-conditioned room, a too-long way. I'm in no mood to stand and contemplate the Pig Bridge and accompanying Pig Shrine, home to a crinkled bronze sow that *gazes down from her high rocky perch on a world much changed since the shrine was built in 1913 to honour the then-queen, born in the Year of the Pig.* I doubt the pig is gazing anywhere. Its face is obscured by heaped-up plastic garlands, garish neon petals, fake pearls. I don't feel like Saranrom Park, either, which holds a memorial to another old queen, one who drowned. I don't want to look at these things and wonder what drew her to them. I don't know, to be honest, why I embark on this same pointless ritual everywhere I go. I walk more briskly, skimming the instructions. Getting to the end of the route will bring me back to the river quicker than turning around, and the sooner I reach the river, the sooner I'll be back at the hotel.

There are only two things left on her list, and the first doesn't even seem to be here. I'm passing the spot where it should be, but like the royal field it seems to have vanished. *Stop in front of the old drum tower and imagine a time when the whole city could be woken by the beating of a single drum.* But there's just another whitewashed wall. She might have got the location wrong – it wouldn't be the first time. Or the tower might be gone, or lurking somewhere, disguised by the passage of time like the paved-over field. I look into the gloom, but can only see the flickering flashlights of men setting up a night-time flea market on the canal bank. Heaps of junk, tools and toys and trinkets in landfill condition, spread out on tarpaulins. Past the glimmer of paste jewellery I can see the walls of a temple, and beyond that the sky screwing itself up into storm-clouds.

The temple is Wat Pho, the last place on the page. Surely there's nothing secret about this one – home of the Reclining Buddha, one of the country's most celebrated attractions. I flick down to see what she has to say.

Siam has long been a thriving trade centre. Chinese junks would come with silk, and buy rice. With a heavier cargo on the homebound journey, they added extra weight to their outward voyages in the form of stone statues. These were left behind, and Thai temples were more than happy to adopt them as decoration, or guardians...

Standing across the street, I can see the shadows dancing behind the temple gate. I hear the muted sound of someone calling in Thai, somewhere inside – it sounds like they're greeting a friend, or bidding them goodnight. It reminds me, too, of her, when we were kids. The way she would call to me from her hiding places in the garden, softly, so that I'd drive myself crazy trying to find her. I cross the road and step through the gate, pay my 50 baht, walk into the temple compound. It's eerie, in the almost-deserted dark. There's a bit of a breeze scuffling about, and a few scattered spits of rain. The smell of dust blooms up from the ground. Apart from the woman in the ticket booth there's no one else here. Whoever was calling is gone, perhaps deeper into the compound – there's another wall ahead, and another behind that. The place like a set of boxes, one inside the other, filled with ballast statues: humans, animals, monsters, with cartoon faces and unreal bodies. The glow of my phone makes the shadows deeper, and I almost jump and drop it when I see the eyes of a temple cat glare at me from under a tree. I shake my head at myself and carry on reading.

If your exploring happens to take place late in the day, Wat Pho at night is a delightfully surreal experience. Seeing the famed temple without crowds, with stray night-breezes gusting through, and stone creatures peering out of the darkness, is like stumbling into an alternate world. I blink at the sudden departure of her usual vagueness. This passage describes the place perfectly. She must have lifted it wholesale from somebody's blog, but the effect of it prickles my skin. I can almost see her, standing at my side, telling one of her stories with eyes shining plasma-screen bright.

It's really trying to rain now, so I duck under some temple eaves. Looking out across the courtyard I see a wall with a gate cut out of it, a half-lit golden spire beyond. The gate is flanked by two stone giants with bulb-noses and portentous hats, parody Europeans with faces carved into inhuman masks framed by abundant ringlets. They get a special mention in my guide:

Stranger than any other temple guardian in the Kingdom, the giants at the gates represent thirteenth century explorer Marco Polo. These statues even manage to sound surreal when described in official guides, as 'four pairs of Marco Polo'.

I feel like I've finally crossed over into the other world, the one I've felt brushing against me all afternoon. The ground hisses, the pale statues look ready to come to life, and I can feel her, leaning on the wall next to me, more than just an echo.

We're all Marco Polos, she says.

CONTRIBUTORS

EDITORS

ANNA MACDONALD is a PhD candidate in Creative Writing at the School of English, Communications and Performance Studies, Monash University, Melbourne. She has published numerous essays in the field of contemporary art, including for the Edinburgh International Festival (2009) and the Venice Biennale (2007). She was an editor of *Verge 2010: Other Places*.

BETHANY NORRIS worked in film and theatre in London and America, before deciding to study creative writing at Warwick. Her poetry has been exhibited with Andrew Motion's at the Victoria and Albert Museum. She has been editing local poetry books, project managing the MA anthology, as well as working as an editor on *Verge*. In her spare time she plays jazz piano and drinks Mojitos by candlelight. Contact: bethania_229@hotmail.com

CATHERINE NOSKE is currently working to complete her doctorate in Creative Writing at Monash University. She has edited *Verge* once before, and has had various pieces published in the anthology in previous years. Her interests lie mainly in contemporary representations of the Australian Gothic, and after completing her studies she intends to move into publishing and editing on a professional basis. She would like to thank all the writers for the effort they have put in – it has made the process of editing a joy!

NICHOLAS TIPPLE first graduated from Warwick in 1999 with a MChem (Hons) degree in chemistry and returned ten years later to do the part-time MA in Writing. He spent the intervening period working in industry, most recently at Sellafield, Cumbria. He still isn't sure how much the experience awakened his mind to the creative process, but the reprocessing micro-community has now become the centre-piece for his first novel. And it features the undead. Contact: nicktipple@yahoo.co.uk

AUTHORS

MICHAELA ATIENZA studied at the University of the Philippines before coming to the University of Warwick to do an MA in English Literature. She lives in the Philippines, where she teaches, attempts poetry, and writes strange short stories. Her work has been published in *Expeditions: The Philippine Graphic/Fiction Awards* (Fully Booked, 2007), and she can be reached at mlj.atienza@gmail.com

CONRAD BIRD lives in the North Yorkshire Moors. He is an obsessive fisherman and travels from Devon to Scotland scrambling over rocks and kelp (he has been cut off by strong tides more than once). In between fishing expeditions he has played music in orchestras, big bands and now plays a wood guitar in a folk band. His writing is affected first-hand by the landscapes and tradition of the folk culture in Northern England and Scotland. His favourite quotation is, 'All music is folk music, I ain't never heard no horse play guitar' (Louis Armstrong). He has just finished a degree in English and Creative Writing at Warwick University.

PETER DAWNCY lives in the Dandenong Ranges east of Melbourne. He has an Arts Degree with majors in English and Philosophy from Monash University. This year he is completing Honours in poetry writing, and for his thesis is studying Philip Hammial's poetry through Gilles Deleuze and Felix Guattari. Peter has been published in *Southerly, Islet, Voiceworks, Mascara Literary Review, LINQ, Steamer!, Ripple, Positive Words, Lot's Wife, Studio, Avid Reader, Verge 2009, 100 Lightnings SF, australianreader.com* and *antisf.com.* He is the winner of the 2010 Monash poetry prize and came second in the 2010 Monash fiction-writing competition. Contact Peter at pghan1@student.monash.edu

CAMERON DICK is a student at Monash University, Melbourne.

SAMUEL DODSON is from the limestone-clad city of Bath and is an English Literature and Creative Writing Undergraduate at Warwick University. He regularly updates his own blog, 'This is not just ordinary blogging' (http://blogs.warwick.ac.uk/samueldodson/) as well as contributing a creative writing wing to Mark Whelan's 'Contemporary and Modern Art' blog (http://contemporaryandmodernart.blogspot.com). Inspired mostly by problematic philosophies, and the minutes which seem like hours yet pass too soon. Often found wasting time procrastinating over thoughts of infinite idealism. Contact: s.dodson_101@hotmail.co.uk

PETER DONALDSON is currently studying Arts at Monash University, focusing on creative writing, philosophy and psychology. Previously a plant-grower, he divides his time between Melbourne and Dimboola (in western Victoria). Contact: pdonaldson@hotmail.com

CAMILLE ECKHAUS is a Law/Arts student at Monash University. She is currently breaking her parents' hearts by putting the law degree on hold in order to undertake an Honours thesis in creative writing, focusing on Gothic Fiction. This is her first publication.

RHIAN GRACO is currently concluding her Bachelor of Arts degree at Monash University, majoring in English, with Journalism and Communication minors. Rhian is hoping to start her graduate career by combining her loves of music and writing to create a career in music journalism, while also pursuing the publication of her creative writing. Contact: rvgra1@student.monash.edu.au

DAVID GREAVES is a student of English Literature and Creative Writing at the University of Warwick. He has been featured alongside Luke Kennard and George Ttoouli in the *New Victoria* anthology commemorating the Odeon cinema in Bradford, and will be releasing his first original publication with the New Fire Tree Press in October. He lives in the North but his accent needs work. Contact: dgreaves822@gmail.com

DR MICHAEL HULSE is an Associate Professor at the University of Warwick. His latest publications are a book of poems, The *Secret History* (Arc), and a translation of Rilke's *The Notebooks of Malte Laurids Brigge* (Penguin Classics). With J M Coetzee and Susannah Moore he is a consultant to Adelaide Writers' Week 2012, and he is a judge of the Günter Grass Foundation's biennial literature award. His co-edited anthology *The Twentieth Century in Poetry* is published by the Random House imprint Ebury this October.

ANNA LEA writes fiction as well as film and television scripts. She wrote a screenplay of her story 'Isaac', which was made into a short film funded by the UK Film Council. She also writes to commission for the BBC, Lonely Planet and others. She teaches screenwriting at the University of Warwick. Contact: annalea@live.co.uk

SOPHIE MACKINTOSH is a recent University of Warwick graduate, where she studied English and Creative Writing. Her writing has appeared in *Pomegranate* and *Spilt Milk* magazine, and in two *Tower Poetry* anthologies. Under the unimaginative pseudonym of 'Sophie Mac', she also released her first EP, 'Apples', in October. She currently lives at home in Pembrokeshire – balancing work as a proof-reader with trying not to kill her parents – but is looking forward to properly starting her post-graduation life as a bona-fide tortured writer, complete with cats, in Glasgow come September. She can be contacted at sophiemackintosh@hotmail.co.uk (when Welsh internet works).

ZOË MCMINN is a reader and writer from Christchurch, Dorset. As well as writing fiction and creative non-fiction, she regularly performs her poetry. Having graduated from the University of Warwick, Zoë now hopes to run creative writing workshops for young people, and learn a new trade. She loves starting off the dancing, fixing things and seeking out experimental music, literature and radio. Contact: z.a.mcminn@gmail.com

NKANDU CHIPALE MWENGE is a Zambian freelance writer and first year Business Science student at Monash South Africa. He has been a band publicist and performance poet. He is currently training under Andrew Miller at the Unity Gallery. The Lake is his first short story. Follow him on twitter @Chipale1 and/or send him an email at nkandu.mwenge@yahoo.com

JON MYCROFT spent nine years stuck in shop demonstration mode before attending Ruskin College in Oxford, England where he read English Literature: Creative Writing and Critical Practice. He is a three-time winner of the Oxford-based *Alistair Whisker Award for Prose,* and taught BA English Literature at Ruskin before joining the Warwick MA Writing Programme. He lives and writes in Leamington Spa, but wasn't really born there. Contact: jmycroft@btinternet.com

AMY NICHOLLS-DIVER is in the last year of a Bachelor of the Arts at Monash University. She has previously been published in *Verge 2010: Other Places, Lot's Wife*, and has contributed to an instruction handbook on water efficiency. Her professed goal is to become a proofreader/copy editor, but she secretly longs to live in a shack and write books of quiet beauty. In 2010/11 Amy was assistant story editor for Celapene Press's *Short and Twisted* story anthology. She writes in an attempt to capture the things that cannot be spoken. For more, email: amy_nicholls_diver@hotmail.com

MATTHEW OWEN is a current student undertaking the University of Warwick's Writing MA. He has had his work published in a range of small magazines and anthologies, and is currently working on his first novel. He is not nearly as cheerless as the story contained herein would suggest. For example, if you asked him whether he liked jazz, he would reply 'yes.' Contact: mattowen23@gmail.com

OSCAR SCHWARTZ is currently writing an Honours thesis in poetics at Monash University, focusing on two contemporary Melbourne poets, Chris Mann and Pi O. His other interests include logic, music and travel. Contact: occi_schwartz@hotmail.com.

SUSAN STANFORD is doing a PhD on the early 20th century female haiku poet Sugita Hisajo. She has published two book of poetry and has been President of the Melbourne Poets Union. This is the second short prose piece she has had in *Verge*.

REBECCA TAMAS has just graduated from the BA course in English Literature and Creative Writing at Warwick and is heading north to do a Creative Writing MSc at Edinburgh. Rebecca is from London, with a bit of Budapest thrown in. She has been published in online and print magazines including *The Cadaverine* and *Dr Hurley's Snake Oil Cure*. She is currently working on her first pamphlet of poetry, about the Large Hadron Collider at Cern. Contact: rebeccatamas22@gmail.com

GEORGIA TOWNLEY delayed her university years by carrying her life on her back for five months around Europe. She swears this was to better understand what she wanted in life, not to drink beer in every city. As a Monash University student, she now splits her time between studying Psychology and English. These two loves often merge in her short stories creating dark humour and intruding into the minds of some very shady characters. Contact: georgia.townley@gmail.com

TORI TRUSLOW was born in Hong Kong, grew up in Thailand, and is currently taking the MA in Writing at Warwick. Her fiction has appeared or is upcoming in *Polluto, Clockwork Phoenix 3, The Draft* and *The Speculative Ramayana Anthology*. She was Writer-in-Residence at Shrewsbury International School from 2008 to 2010, and is hoping to continue working in schools as well as finishing her first novel. Find her on the web at http://toritruslow.com

TYMEK WOODHAM started his creative life as a songwriter, although it was a terrible day when he realised that melody-making was a completely alien concept. He started focusing on words and thus began an immense fascination with poetry. Since enrolling in the English Literature and Creative Writing course at Warwick University, Tymek has broadened his scope somewhat to experiment with different forms and genres of writing, such as 'collage-writing', typographical art and nonsense poetry. 'Smoke' is his first published piece, an experiment with multi-form expression, attempting to bring to life an under-reported topic in world news.

ACKNOWLEDGEMENTS

MANY PEOPLE HAVE contributed to realising *Verge 2011: The Unknowable*. We would like to thank, in particular, Associate Professor Chandani Lokuge (Monash University), Professor David Morley and Professor Maureen Freely (University of Warwick) for making an international, cross-university edition of *Verge* possible. We are grateful to the School of English, Communications and Performance Studies, especially to Lucretia Blanchard, and the Centre for Postcolonial Writing at Monash, as well as the Writing Programme at the University of Warwick for their support.

Verge 2011: The Unknowable is an outcome of the Monash-Warwick Strategic Funding Initiative for Joint Research and Education. This is the seventh edition of *Verge*, and this year we have introduced a number of new initiatives. For the first time, *Verge 2011* includes submissions from two universities, Monash and the University of Warwick. We are excited to present here some of the best new writing from students in Australia and Britain. In addition, contributors and editors have benefited greatly from the advice of referees: Associate Professor Anne Brewster, Dr Elin-Maria Evangelista, Dr Melinda Harper, Professor Trevor Harris, Dr John Hawke, Professor Sue Kossew, Professor Lyn Mccredden, Dr Helen MacDonald, Professor Stephen Muecke, Dr Simone Murray, Dr Tom Petsinis, and Associate Professor Kate Rigby.

We would also like to thank Charlotte Lester for her assitance in copy-editing; Michael Noske for his last-minute efforts in typesetting; and the team at Monash University Publishing who have published *Verge* for the first time this year, and been a huge help throughout the process.

Thanks also go to the team at the Melbourne Writers Festival for their assistance in launching the anthology.

We would like to thank Peter Blegvad for his wonderful cover art. We could not have hoped for a better image to encapsulate the spirit of 'the Unknowable'; and further thanks to Dr. Michael Hulse for his generosity in writing a foreword.

Finally, thank you to all the writers included in this volume, and to all of those who submitted such an exciting range of creative responses to this year's theme.

We sincerely hope you enjoy reading this anthology as much as we have enjoyed working on it.

Anna MacDonald
Bethany Norris
Catherine Noske
Nicholas Tipple